WAR'S UNCONQUERED CHILDREN SPEAK

Ideas into Books®
W E S T V I E W
P.O. Box 605
Kingston Springs, TN 37082
www.publishedbywestview.com

ISBN 978-1-62880-099-9

Second edition, October 2016

The author gratefully acknowledges permission to reprint the text and illustrations included in "A Syrian teenager escapes from war-torn Aleppo," courtesy www.rescue.org, used by permission of Paul Donohoe, Senior Media Officer—Syria Regional Response, International Rescue Committee (IRC).

Good faith efforts have been made to trace copyrights on materials included in this publication. If any copyrighted material has been included without permission and due acknowledgment, proper credit will be inserted in future printings after notice has been received.

Printed in the United States of America on acid free paper.

Dedication of the Second Edition:

It was my good fortune in 1977 to meet the remarkable Alice Cobb. I was young and naive, fresh out of college, and she was less young and more experienced. She had a lot to teach me. Between that meeting and her death in 1995, we talked. A lot.

The primary subject to which she kept returning—time after time—was this volume. She grieved its loss as one might grieve a stillborn child, for it had gone out of print, the print run had mysteriously disappeared, and she had not a single copy left. She talked about it so many times that notwithstanding the years since, I have always remembered its title—in spite of the fact that I never even got to read the book. She always referred to it as "the best thing I [she] ever wrote."

Alice's longing for a copy of her own was so profound that it soon became my mission to find her one. I frequently requested it from used book stores and advertised for it on obscure used book lists, but with no success. Even after her death I kept looking for it almost out of habit, whenever it came to mind.

And then, in the fall of 2016, yet another search found it, available on Interlibrary Loan from the Jean & Alexander Heard Library of Vanderbilt University. When I received it, thanks to the South Cheatham Public Library in Kingston Springs, Tennessee, I was thrilled to discover the copyright date was 1953, a time when the protected period for books which had been registered but not renewed was only twenty-eight years. I searched copyright records and was able to confirm the original registration in one of the '53 yearbooks, but no mention of it could be found in either the 1981 or 2009 records, the years it would have been eligible for registration renewal. After thirty-nine years of searching, Alice's lost writing was not only in my hands but also in the public domain.

And so, dear Alice, I dedicate this second edition to you. Here is your "best thing." Sorry it took so long.

M.C. Nelson, *Ideas into Books*® WESTVIEW

Though Alice Cobb's *War's Unconquered Children Speak* was written in the mid-twentieth century, the effects of war on refugee children are the same now—in the twenty-first—as they were then. Children suffer and survive—and even thrive—no matter what war's time or place.

The publisher is grateful for the opportunity to include the following twenty-first century story from Syria as a preface to the Second Edition.

Shattered by the death of her parents and younger sister, 16–year–old Hiba* somehow found the strength to lead her brothers to safety in Jordan. Thank you to Paul Donohoe, Senior Media Officer–Syria Regional Response, International Rescue Committee (IRC), for permission to include her recollections of the journey and her drawings of life in Syria.

The following was reprinted from the IRC website, www.rescue.org.

October 11, 2016:

Thousands of children in war-torn Aleppo are trapped without food, water or medical care as the city collapses from many months of intense aerial bombing.

The carnage took the lives of 16–year–old Hiba's* parents and sister, but against all odds she was able to escape to Jordan with her three younger brothers.

The war in Syria spares no one. Many children have lost their families – left to embark on a journey to safety alone without any protection. Hiba and her siblings waited three months at the International Rescue Committee center for unaccompanied minors in Azraq while aid workers took the steps necessary to reunite them with relatives already in Jordan.

Hiba shared her heartrending story with us:

In 2011, the war in Syria started. We left our neighborhood in Aleppo for another we thought was safe. But a missile hit the bakery where my dad worked and he died. We spent two years mourning; there wasn't much joy left in our lives.

But my mother made us feel like life could be normal again, and that there's hope in this world. She took us to another area, which was safer. We stayed there for two years. We could come and go whenever we wanted. There was a strong sense of community; people were united. You would feel as comfortable out on the streets as in your own home. I used to go to school also; I studied until 10th grade.

I have fond memories of my father; I consider our time together to be the best days of my life. I remember one time—it was during the month of Ramadan—after Iftar [breaking the fast meal]—my dad decided to take us on a trip. He took us to the amusement park and we had such a good time.

On the way home, he opened the car's rooftop and my sister and I stuck our heads out of the window. We stayed up until 4am! Imagine, it was that safe that we could stay up so late and nobody would bother us.

The bombing

It was Feb. 21. My younger sister, Ghazal, was playing with her friend out on the street, just in front of my aunt's shop. I was in our house alone. My mother was having coffee at our neighbor's house and my brothers were out playing with their friends.

When the bombing happened, I passed out because a door fell on me. A man pulled me out, and when I woke up, everything had changed. My home was destroyed.

I went running to look for my mother, and I found her and my two brothers. My mother started screaming and went looking for my sister. I was told to stay behind.

A second bombing killed my mother, along with my sister, who was only in first grade. At 12am, we found my third brother alive.

My mother was a strong woman. She would provide for us. She mourned my father's death for three years, but people told her that it's a long time to mourn. So she stopped wearing black and started wearing brighter clothes. But then she was killed.

The journey

When my mother and sister died, my brothers and I stayed at my uncle's house for a month. After that, my grandparents asked us to stay with them in Amman.

I couldn't bear to stay in Syria. It kept reminding me of what I lost—it drove me crazy. My brothers and I chose to leave Syria all together.

We made the journey to Jordan alone. My aunt helped us get a taxi, which dropped us off close to the border. We walked to the berm [a no-man's land between Syrian and Jordan].

During our journey, we were supporting each other. My oldest brother, Mousa, 15, and I took care of our younger brothers Ahmad, 14, and Abdo, 12. My brothers are all short-tempered ever since our days in Syria; they can't handle too much pressure.

They're not easy to deal with, but they're my brothers and I have to take care of them. I usually try to advise them and give them direction on what's right and what's wrong. If they don't listen, I don't push them.

I only brought pictures and a piece of clothing that belonged to my mother, which still carries her scent. I also brought my little sister's pajamas that she was wearing before she changed and went to play the day she died.

It's not a nice place—the berm. It's a vast desert with so much sand and many tents. It looked like half of Syria was there. Once we arrived, I went to the guards and told them we're alone. They looked at our papers, then at us, and immediately let us cross [the border into Jordan].

There was an officer there who was very kind to us; I will never forget his kindness. He gave my brothers and I clothes, food and money, and found us a place to stay with very nice people.

He told us that we will be going to a better place tomorrow, and it was true. We met people from the IRC and then went to the child-protection reception area—the nicest place ever.

The trauma

I used to sit next to my mother's grave and found comfort in that. I cried throughout the whole journey to Jordan. I would think back and regret ever fighting with my sister. If I knew she was going to die, I would have never fought with her.

When we got to the child–protection reception area, I was surprised that I was still standing on my own two feet. I thought I would never be able to get over of my grief. But I found that the IRC staff, and the other girls there, are nice people.

I started drawing and joining in activities like Zumba and theater [workshops] to help me forget about my misery. I don't like sitting alone without anything to do because everything comes back to me … it's hard for me.

When I feel pressured, I don't reveal my sadness or take out my anger at people; I let it out by drawing. I take a pencil and paper and let out everything I have inside. When I finish my drawings, I look at them and see memories. And I think— is this how I was? I should go back to the way I used to be.

But I felt like my mental state was better at the IRC, because I had my friends around me and we would play and joke around.

My uncle and grandmother would visit us at the reception area. I was so happy to see someone related to me—it kept me hopeful. There are still people in this world that I love.

The reunion

After three months at the reception area, we were able to stay with our grandparents. They told us that we would be moving to Amman, a nicer place. I had mixed feelings; I was both happy and sad.

The first two days in Amman, I felt uncomfortable. I missed my friends at the reception area, and I started thinking again. I kept thinking that I would never see my mother's grave again.

Sometimes my brothers and I get bored, so we start fighting. I don't like that. I don't want us to be a source of noise in the house. I keep telling my brothers that everything can be solved peacefully but, you know, they're boys, they want to show their muscles.

My grandparents are extremely good to us; they pamper us. They have enrolled us in school — we started in

September! My wish is to finish high school and get my bachelor's degree and work as a nurse.

In Syria, I spent two months shadowing nurses. It actually made me a stronger person when I saw dead people on the street—without heads, legs, arms or insides.

I am relieved because my brothers and I are safe, but I miss my family. We left behind so many memories; we left behind a life and our country. The hardest thing to lose is one's parents and country, and we lost them all.

But I have my dreams. There's still hope for me to live a good life with an education. My wish is for my mother and father to be proud of me.

Names were changed for privacy reasons

The IRC's child protection team works in partnership with the United Nations refugee agency (UNHCR) and the U.N. Children's Fund (UNICEF).

Please note: Hiba's drawings are found on the cover and on the pages following page xii, where the original illustrations for *War's Unconquered Children Speak* were located.

War's Unconquered Children Speak

by

ALICE COBB

with an introduction by Sophia L. Fahs

THE BEACON PRESS   BOSTON

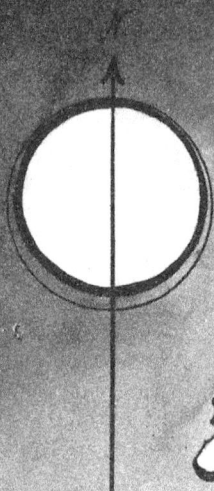

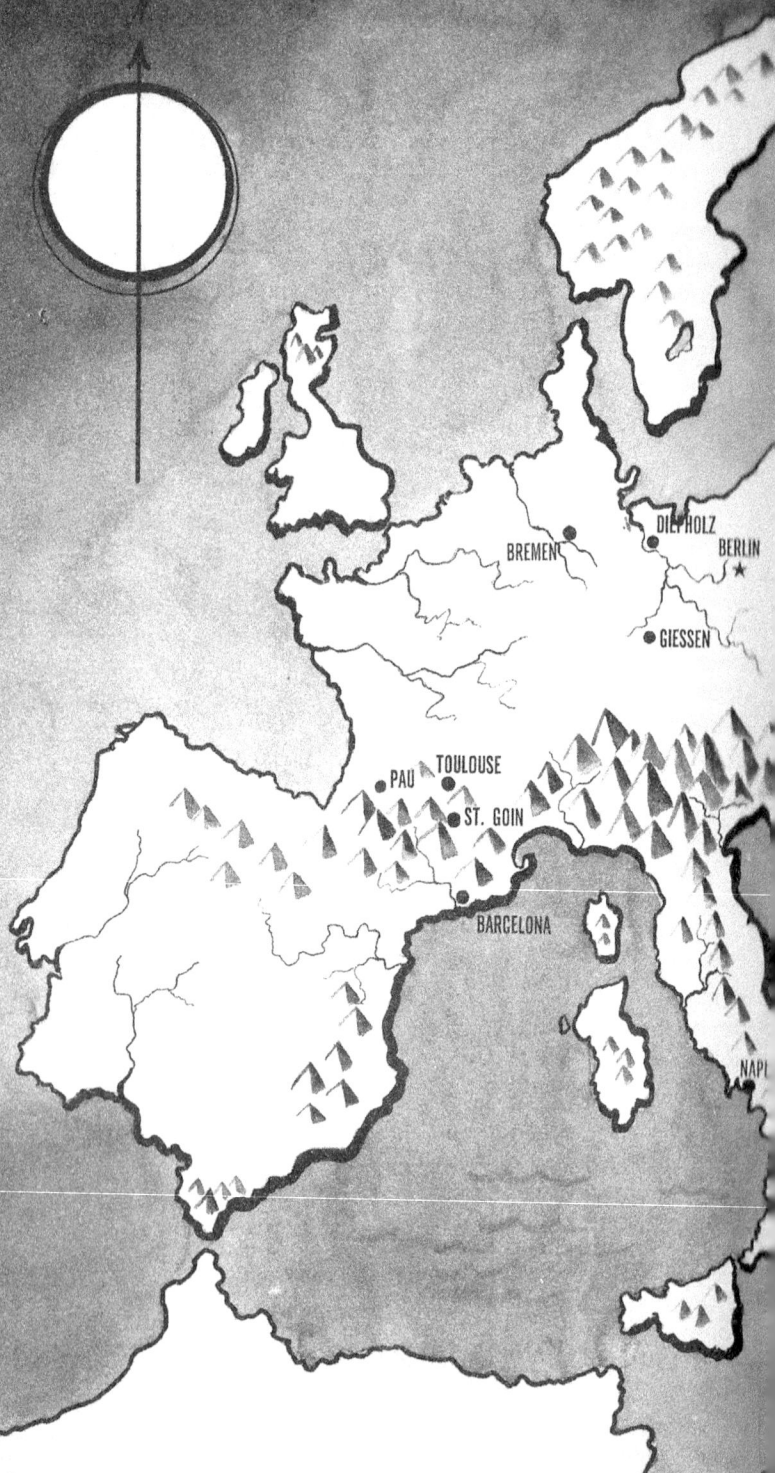

Printed in U.S.A.

Contents

WAR'S UNCONQUERED CHILDREN SPEAK

FROM GREECE

FROM THE MIDDLE EAST

FROM ITALY

vi Contents

FROM FRANCE

FROM GERMANY

FROM FINLAND

Introduction

These moving first-hand narrative sketches are all true. All the people are real. All the places are right there on the map. In some cases names have been changed because use of true names might endanger relatives.

The project was born in the imagination of the author, who wished to see and understand the problems of the displaced people of the world through their own eyes and feelings. She wanted to meet in person some of these " children of war " and to talk with them. To accomplish this, she made a four-month journey through nine countries of Europe and the Middle East. She sought children and their families who had been obliged to leave their homes, who had lost relatives and friends, who were living in ruined villages and cities, in orphanages, settlements, camps, or newly built towns. She found them in Lebanon, Syria, Jordan, and in the Gaza strip, now under Egyptian mandate. She found them in Greece and Italy, in France, Germany, and Finland. She talked with these " children of war." She listened to their stories, kept notes of what she saw and heard. The people assured her that they were willing to have her readers know how they thought — and felt.

The realism of some of these sketches may disturb certain people who dream of a peaceful world. But we are counting on their reaching many people who not only are familiar with some of the tragic facts of the world, but also may perhaps have a fresher and more hopeful attitude toward them than some others who have grown tired and numb. Readers of these stories will find plenty of tonic for good hard thinking. They will feel themselves growing in breadth of sympathy even while debating the issues. And none will fail to be moved by the recurring revelation of human resilience, which makes people able to face loss with courage — even to laugh, to love, to sing in the face of tragedy.

This is not a book of stories told primarily to elicit worn clothes for the poverty-stricken, or food packages for the starving (desperately needed as these services are). Philanthropy on a larger scale than has ever yet been dreamed of is called for. For a long time to come there seems to be little hope of meeting the tragic physical needs of all our human relatives. That the reading of this book will result in the doing of something concretely beneficial seems as natural as human kindness. The organizations that are eager for assistance are listed in the appendix.

But what matters even more than philanthropy is how we *feel* toward these persons. What we can *do* for them seems infinitesimal; yet in the long run how we *think* of them — whether we include them in our imaginations, whether we can identify ourselves with them in our feelings — does matter. It matters first of all to ourselves, for our own healing; and it matters also to the future of our civilization.

How large an outlook on human existence are we willing to gain? How intelligent are we determined to be? How much sympathy are we able to feel? The leadership in the planning for these world-wide relationships will soon be transferred to younger minds. They should be more understanding than their elders. They must learn to diagnose the psychological sicknesses of nations as well as those of individuals, and to discover successful means of healing.

The book might have been labeled " lessons in international

relations," but we could not call it that because we confess we are not sure what " lessons " should be drawn from these life histories. We are living in a world where millions of people have had their whole outlook on life and death, God and the universe, shattered by war's destruction and cruelties. Many are trying to clear these spiritual ruins and to build a new meaning into existence. For the time being some are so absorbed in hatreds that their energies are consumed, while others, perhaps less threatened, have won wisdom, and even tenderness, through their sorrows.

The tragedies of real life touch us with a depth of poignancy that even the greatest fiction can seldom produce. This is perhaps because we cannot escape feeling some responsibility for trying to change the outcome. These stories are unfinished as all life is unfinished. The solutions are still to be achieved.

This book has in it a great deal of tragedy. Terrifying and complex problems are here, and the kinds of emotions we tend to want to hide in the dark. " The stories are very moving " — so a number of readers have already said — " yet they are also very beautiful." When one discovers even occasionally the bloom of a mature sympathy, and the brightness of gaiety, springing up out of the mire of cruel experience, the miracle of it lends a glory to all humanity and makes our own less reasonable hatreds seem almost ridiculous. These stories are for our own healing as well as for the healing of others.

It seems truly remarkable that, in spite of the barrier of language in most countries, Miss Cobb was able to win such confidence from those she interviewed that they were able and willing to reveal themselves naturally and vividly to her. Some skill in shorthand and a reporter's knack are partially responsible, combined with her own native talent as a writer.

Some of the questions she asked must have been painful to answer. But almost always the people she talked with accepted her questions in the spirit in which she asked them, and she believes they answered honestly.

The project was encouraged and partially supported by a number of people and organizations and even by governments. The author was entertained and guided in all her visits by representatives of the organizations especially interested in the localities where she went. About thirty-three different voluntary and governmental agencies are represented. Without the assistance of all of these persons and organizations, the project could never have been accomplished. Neither could it have even been launched without the perseverance, hard work and deep purposefulness of the author.

Since the book is non-partisan and religiously non-sectarian, it is appropriate for very wide use. I recommend it to anyone, of any age beyond childhood, who cares to see human problems dramatized in the experiences of real people, who wants to broaden his understanding and to deepen his sympathies, who is willing to listen when the children of war themselves speak.

Sophia L. Fahs

A Note About the Author

The Italians were " born to sing " — so says the author. Of Alice Cobb herself one might say, " She was born to write." She loves words, she is thrilled with ideas, she enjoys even the mechanical process of putting words on paper. But her real absorption is with people — all kinds of people — and her love of writing is born of a longing to understand and to interpret human problems.

Ever since her college and theological seminary days, she has been seeking the kinds of professional opportunities that would bring her in contact with people. She spent several years at the Pine Mountain Settlement School in Harlan County, where she was deeply concerned with the problems and with the people of the Kentucky mountains. For three years she supervised a settlement in one of the worst slums of Brooklyn. For another three years she was State Community Organization Consultant for the Kentucky Division of Child Welfare, in a position where she met all kinds of people and continually practiced dynamic group leadership.

Alice Cobb has an experimental attitude of mind that constantly lures her on to new and different experiences. She tested out permissive and exploratory ways of teaching with a class of boys and girls in the Riverside Church School, New York City; ten years later, she still tells with enthusiasm how those children taught religion to *her*. This same yearning to learn from direct experience has given her a zest for travel, and often she has spent vacations or other periods in some form of educational adventure abroad. For one semester she was on the staff of the Brickwall School in Northiam, Sussex, England. One summer she visited the Danish folk school in Hans Christian Andersen's home town of Odense. Another summer she traveled with a group of ministers and archaeologists through Palestine, Italy, and Greece.

This is Miss Cobb's first real book — so she would say. But she admits that once she collected and edited a book of Kentucky mountain folk tales and historical materials, which was published by the Pine Mountain School. While working with the Kentucky Child Welfare Division she wrote the Kentucky report for the Mid-Century White House Conference for Children and Youth.

The project which has brought this book into being was born in Miss Cobb's own creative imagination. She wanted to meet in person some children who were refugees from war, to talk with them, to try to understand their problems and their adjustments directly — and to pass this knowledge on to other people.

S.L.F.

cover photo:

This is a bombing that took away many beloved people. I was there; I saw it happen. I can't begin to describe what these people meant to me. This is a mother who is trying to protect her child, but can't. I didn't draw a house; I drew safety in a mother's arms. Next to it, I wrote a little poem about Syria. It reads: "A person who lost his gold can find it in the gold market, and a person who lost a lover will soon forget him, but a person who lost his country, where will he find it?"

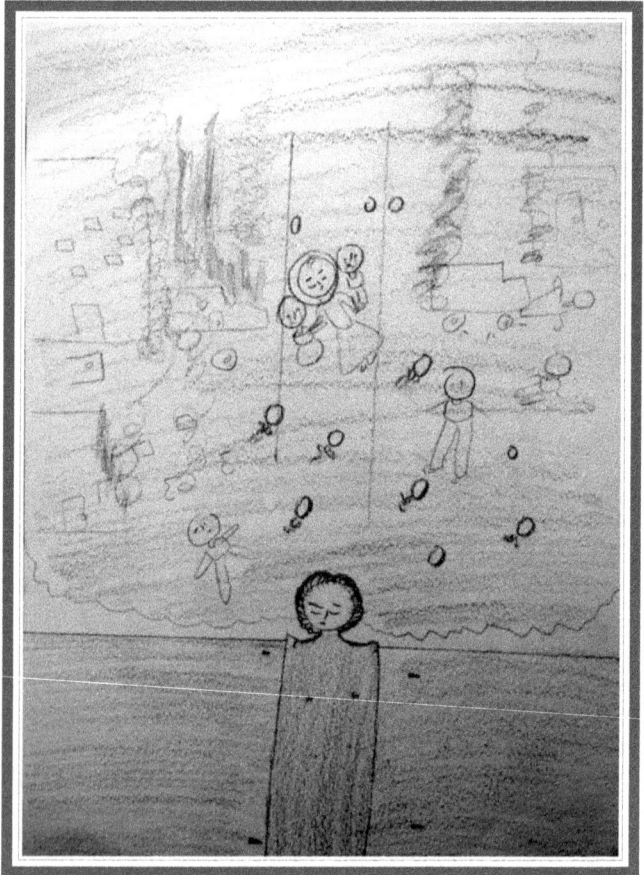

My brother told me that he dreamt of the bombing. So I drew him, how he's sleeping and dreaming of the bombing. I showed it to him and he started laughing at me; he told me that this wasn't his dream. His dream was more intense.

Photo: IRC

We went to buy new clothes for Eid. I remembered my mother; how we would buy new clothes for Eid together. I drew the children's clothing shop, and the mother and her child, but when I started drawing myself, I couldn't finish. I flipped the page and left the drawing incomplete.

This is my grandmother. My brothers and I were sitting around her and she started telling us stories about my dad when he was a kid. My grandmother started crying remembering him and we started crying too.

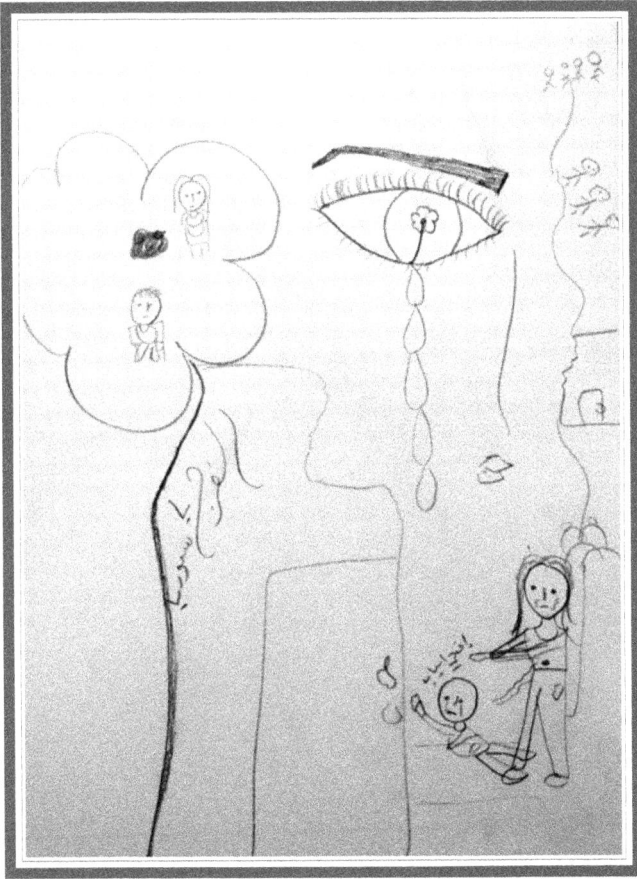

Photo: IRC

I drew how [the war] all started with a revolution, and then came the bombings and military planes, then people started dying and the cemeteries got bigger. A girl witnessed it all and has the key that will open the door to peace. But she is wounded and the boy with her is about to die. He says, "Open the door." The eye has a flower, which represents Syria, and it's crying. The people in the flower are the people of Syria waiting for peace to prevail. It says, "Everything will be good again, Syria."

FROM GREECE

CHAPTER ONE

This Little Piece of Earth

I arranged to make my study of the Greek people and their prob-
lems through two colleges, Anatolia in Thessalonika, almost at the
northern tip of Greece and near the Yugoslav border, and Pierce Col-
lege in Elleniko, which is close to Athens in the south. The Congrega-
tional Christian Service Committee has headquarters in both places.
Both colleges were occupied during the last war by the German army.
Some of the students remember well the evacuation and return. And
in Thessalonika the young children can remember the 1947–1949
civil war when the Communist guerilla raiders attacked the villages
and carried away many of their companions to Yugoslavia, Albania,
Bulgaria, and even to Soviet Russia.

The first days in Greece were confusing. I wondered how
to begin learning the Greek story in one brief throw, knowing
it couldn't be done, and yet feeling desperately determined
not to lose a single one of those first quick, hard impressions.

There were the contrasts: the witches' brew of ancient and
modern, Christianity and vestiges of ancient paganism living
together, the sharply differing political views, the very mock-
ery of the brilliant sunshine that ought to have been warm
but had no warmth in it. For Greece in April was a frozen
goddess, lovely to look at and cruelly cold. I was moved by
the intense beauty, the extremes of color, the blue sky, the
dazzling yellow, red, and purple profusion of flowers, the
green grass and leaves, white houses, all sharply clear-cut in
the bright pure air. But the cold wind never stopped blowing.

In Greece, I was told, nine out of every ten people one meets

are " refugees " from some war, and more than half of these
are now living in homes which they do not consider permanent.

There are large groups of Armenians who fled from Turkey
into Greece to escape Turkish hostility some years ago.   There
are thousands of Greeks who were born in what is now Turkey, and who fled to Greece after the Turkish revolution in
1921.   And there are many other Greeks who lost their homes,
jobs and possessions during World War II when Italy and
Germany occupied Greece.   There are still others who had
their homes destroyed by American bombs.   During the civil
war which followed the world war, nearly a thousand villages
were ruined and evacuated.   In fact for centuries there has
hardly been a time when Greece was not either involved in a
war, or endeavoring — as she is now — to recover from war.

Gradually I began to sort out problems as I saw them,
learning more about Greece's history of wars, and trying to
realize the terrible cost of this almost continuous destruction.

The remarkable thing is that today the Greek countryside
presents to a casual observer a serene and orderly appearance.
One sees few ruins without actually hunting for them.   The
Greek farmer, who yesterday was a soldier and tomorrow may
be a soldier again, goes about his planting and plowing, trims
his bushes and cuts his weeds and whitewashes his house, even
though it may be a temporary mud hut or a stone building
made by his own hands.

I could not take casually the mother, for instance, who went
about her work in the kitchen or the shop, singing a Greek
song, while I knew her mind must be constantly keeping company with her boy who was six, and is now nine, living behind
some iron curtain.   Or — even worse — not knowing whether
he was there.   I kept trying to remember that practically
everybody I met in Greece had had the experience once at

least of leaving his home, or seeing his village evacuated, and losing everything he owned. Most of them had found new homes for themselves, only to be dispossessed yet again. They seemed to have adapted themselves somehow to being refugees.

In Macedonia, which of all Greece was hardest hit throughout, I kept trying to remember that this neat and pleasant land had been ravaged by invading armies time and time again over hundreds of years, and much of it scarred and burned by guerrilla invasions, as well as mutilated during the Italian and German occupations.

In the city of Athens in the south, there is continuous bustle and clang, the crowds stream in and out through the shop doors, the ancient ruins gleam in the moonlight, the outdoor coffee places are jammed with people out-talking each other. All over the country the people are great talkers, and I was told that wherever three Greeks get together one finds three political parties waging a campaign. " But praise God we can talk," said my friend Mrs. Haniatou. " When Greek people cannot talk any more, then Greece is truly in peril."

Recovery then is the keynote and the theme in poverty-stricken Greece. It is coming. And it is coming only partly through help from Western Europe and from America via the Marshall Plan program. It is coming largely because of the pride and indomitable will of the Greek people to survive. One has the feeling that they could not possibly permit themselves to die.

As I sorted out all these reactions and much information which was generously offered to me along my way, I learned to know a great many people. I found the Greeks as warm and soft of heart as their country is cold and rocky. I found them as kind as they are brave, and as gay as they could possibly be sad. It was in southern Greece that I learned to know Mrs. Flora Haniatou, who came to represent for me the whole history and life and spirit of her country. She was herself a refugee from Smyrna after the Turkish revolution, had been active in all parts of Greece during the second world war, and was a leading social and community worker with children following the war. She is now dietitian at Pierce College, but she is more than that. I don't know that there is a name for her real position, but Miss Nichol, the president of the college, calls her " The Foundation and the Rock."

Mrs. Haniatou, with her kindness, her humor, her independence, her bottomless fund of knowledge and her enthusiasm and loyalty, to me simply *was* Greece.

She laughed, she sang, she danced, she sparkled, she wept, and she talked and talked and talked. In Attica, Macedonia, the Islands she seemed to know every village from the farthest north to the farthest south. She seemed to have relatives almost everywhere, and where she had no relatives she had close friends. She knew all about the king and the queen and the palace guards. She knew the soldiers, the teachers and the farmers. She knew the government officials. Greek history, ancient and modern, poured from her heart and lips in a stream that confused and confounded me. I felt she must have been present at every battle fought in Greece during the past thirty years. " We Greeks! " she would say in a deprecating but loving way; and when Flora Haniatou said " We Greeks! " I knew that she referred to the most remarkable, delightful, resourceful and worthwhile people in the whole world.

She was deeply interested and more than a little concerned about my purpose in visiting her country, and I think somewhat dubious about my qualifications for the job. " It is a pity I can't do it for you," she said frankly but without haughtiness. I wished that she could.

" You will forgive me if I seem too proud, too anxious for

my country," she said. " We Greeks are so poor. We are not very well educated and we have such a little land, all mountains and rivers and islands and seas. No one can make a good living farming or in any other way. But poor as it is and small and placed at the heart of all the trouble in the world — this little piece of earth we love so very much! "

And so it is with a warm feeling of gratitude and responsibility to my friend that I have prepared the stories from Greece, and with the hope that they will express, at least in part, the sincere admiration I have for that indomitable will to live which has so long preserved for the Greeks their " little piece of earth."

CHAPTER TWO

I, Sophia Alexiou

*I met Sophia at the home of President Compton of Anatolia Col-
lege in Thessalonika. When I asked her to tell me some things which
I might perhaps write in a book to help others understand some of the
problems of the Greeks, she said she would be quite willing to answer
all my questions — " if they were not too difficult." She was rather
pleased, which is not to say flattered, to think that she might be " in a
book," and talked to me steadily for the whole of two bright but
chilly mornings. She spoke carefully in her best English " for the
American people," as she said, all the while watching the shorthand
notes go down in my book with a great deal of curiosity and obvious
respect. I am sorry the reader of this story cannot recall with it, as
I do, the pleasant cadences of Sophia's soft, clipped English, the light
and shadow which came by turns into her warm dark eyes as she
recalled her childhood — and the glorious beauty of Macedonian
spring which was all around us as setting for our conversations.*

*Her name has been changed, and in writing the things she told me
I have condensed much and added a little for clarity. But I have tried
to follow Sophia's gentle manner of speaking, and to keep close to
the spirit of her words. Perhaps she will read the story herself some
day, and I should be sorry to have her disappointed.*

I, Sophia Alexiou, am a Greek, and I am sixteen years old.
Can I remember all that has happened to me in sixteen years?
It seems like a long time. When my mother was well she
used to say the years seem long only when one is young. She
said that when one grows old they fly like minutes and are
gone. Then perhaps I am young, although sometimes I feel
very old, or perhaps the years were long to me because so
many things happened in them. Some things were good.

Many were bad. When my mother was well she used to say, " It is better to be strong for the hard times. But always it is best to be ready also for the good times. They will surely come."

Well, I will tell you something about my earliest childhood. That was good, I think. I was born in Florina, and Florina is a pretty town and a big one too, on the northern border of my country. There are mountains all around Florina, and I think there were quite a great many people there when I was a child.

My father was a musician in the band of the army, and I can remember the uniform he wore. He was a very great musician, I believe, and played many instruments. He played on the accordion, and the clarinet, and the saxophone and the piano, and on a small organ we had at home. My father would play and my mother would sing, and I would try to sing too. We were happy. My uncle was in the next house to us, and my grandfather worked at the army station, but only part of the time for he was old. We had a great deal of money and our family had two fine houses. My grandmother lived in the house with my father and mother, and we had three floors with many many rooms and windows, there in Florina.

Always my father said, " Our Sophia will go to school. Sophia will be a scholar."

Now I do not know why he said it because then not very many even of the rich girls in Greece would be going to school for long. A little knowledge to read, a little knowledge to write, and that was enough for a girl to be married and to keep her house. But my father said it was a new world, and in this new world all must be educated, men and women also, not only to read and to write, but to be scholars. The new world, he said, will be harder than the old.

My mother said, " It has always been hard in Greece."

" But it will be harder still," my father said.

Well I think you will want to know what a small Greek girl in a mountain village of Macedonia might be thinking. Maybe it is the same as the small American girl.

I would look at the mountains around Florina, like a wall, and I asked my father what was on the other side of the mountains.

" In this direction," my father would say, " there is Greece, and you must always think of Greece with love and pride because it is your country where you were born.   And here in the north we are near to Mount Olympus which our people used to think was the place where Zeus lived, and Athene, and Aphrodite, and all the others."   And he told me the stories of the gods.   " And in the south," he said, " there is Athens where that wise man Socrates once lived."   And he told me about Socrates and Plato and Aristotle and other wise men of Greece.

Then I would look in the other direction, and I would say, " What is on the other side of the mountains *that* way? " and my father would tell me that over there was Yugoslavia. " It is another country," he said.   " It is not your homeland."

And I would think, " Someday I will go and see what is on the other side of the mountains.   I will go and see Athens, and perhaps I will go in the other direction to the north, and then I will see Yugoslavia too."   That would be very wonderful because no one except my father had been to any other country or to Yugoslavia.   I imagined what the people would look like there and how queer they would be, but when I asked my father he said they looked like us.   He said they spoke a different language.   He said I would not be able to understand Serbian.

I asked my father why this should be, but he did not know,

only that different countries often have different languages. I tried to imagine people speaking in so many different tongues, all saying the same thing. I had a game. I made queer noises with my lips and said, " Now I speak Serbian! " and then I made noises and said, " Now it is French I speak! " or " Now it is English! " — until at last my mother asked if I would be so kind as to speak in Greek for a time because all the other languages were making her like a deaf person.

Well, I thought, I will really speak all those languages one day and I will go across the mountains and I will visit all the countries of the world, and I will know the English people, and the German people. I will know everybody in the world. That was a long time ago, and I have not visited any other country, but people from many countries have come to Greece. Is it not strange!

Well, the first I saw were the Germans, but I did not see them very much, until later. They made the goose's step as I remember. But I was very small, and we went away almost at once.

This is what happened, and this I can remember. This I cannot forget because sometimes I am dreaming of the bombs. The first bomb fell on the house next to where I lived. It was the house of my uncle. My mother and my grandmother ran out to look, but my mother sent me back. And that house was burning, and there were six houses burning. There was another bomb then. My mother screamed and held me, and she cried that we would be killed. But nothing happened then because that bomb did not explode. It was there on the street, and when we walked we went far around away from it. My mother punished me because I wished to go up close and look at it.

Then all was quiet. The airplanes went away, and it was very quiet and the houses were burning.

Then my mother said, " Well, we must go."

My grandmother wished to go into the burning house where my uncle was, but my mother made her come away, and we went to Evia, where my grandfather had a house.

I was sorry to go because I could not take anything, not a plaything in my hand, except the chain with the locket that has the saint's picture. That brings luck!

I was sorry too because my father was with the army and we must go without my father. So there was my grandmother and my grandfather who was too old to be a soldier and my mother and there was I, a small child. We rode on a bus, standing up with many people, all the way to Athens, because the Germans were coming. I thought I would see Socrates in Athens, but it was a great city and there were crowds of people and we spoke to no one, only to find the way and to hurry and hurry. All the people were hurrying. Then we went on a small boat to Evia.

Now Evia is an island. Greece has many islands and I cannot tell you exactly where it is, but Evia is not so far away from Athens. There were only thirty families living in that village where my grandfather's house was.

But it was pretty although there were not any mountains. Grapes grew there, and we lived in a stone house. We had a storehouse for vegetables. I knew some children there on Evia and they were ignorant children. They had never seen any other place.

" Do you know what is on the other side of that water? " I asked them. I told them there was Athens and there was Greece, and there was Florina, and then there was Yugoslavia where the people spoke a different language. But when my mother looked across the sea she would say, " There is trouble. There is much trouble! "

My mother was not very well then.

There was not a school in that little village, it was so small.

But I was a big girl and my mother said, " Sophia must go to school. Her father has said it, and it must be." There was a school in another village but I must walk an hour to the school. Every day an hour, and in the winter when it was cold I cried, but my mother said it must be because it was my father's wish. I went until after the third grade.

Then the letter came, and letters did not come very often. My mother was frightened. She waited to open it. But after she read the letter she said " Sophia, you must be a woman now. Listen. Your father is dead! "

So my mother was very sick, and maybe she was about to die, but she was religious. There was only a little church, and the priest came once every month and she would pray. She would always pray to go back to Florina.

We did go back to Florina after the war with the Germans was over, and my grandfather was dead too before we went away from Evia. My grandmother went with us because she had no one else of her own. We took the boat to Athens, and then we went on the bus back to our village.

It was the same, but it was not the same. The big houses were gone. Both the houses we had were gone, and there was no place to live. Some of the people my mother knew gave us rooms at different times. We slept on the floor sometimes. And then my mother must build a little house.

We had not much money, but we found some things we had owned before. There was a plate in one house and in one place we found a chair and it was like that. Our friends who had saved them brought them to my mother. But most of the things had been taken by strangers so that we never found them again. In the church was the little organ my father had played. My mother took it and sold it for money to build a house. She did not cry very often but she cried when she sold the little organ.

The new house was a small one. It had one room and one

window and one door. There was no floor at all, only the ground. "Well, it is a place to live," my mother said. "This is our home."

But it was cold and my mother was sick.

You might ask what a girl ten years old would think. There was not much thinking, I believe. It is when you have time and when you are alone or when you are not afraid that you think. There was much to do. I was always in the house with my grandmother and my mother because my mother would have me close to her except when I went to school. And I was always afraid. You are always afraid, I believe, when these things once have happened. Perhaps that is not quite true. I am not afraid now. Not always. But perhaps I am afraid I shall dream.

But it was at once that the guerrilla war began, and then there was no peace or rest any more. We heard that the Communists were coming to take the villages, and every night my mother said, " If God is willing we are alive tomorrow," and every morning she said, " God has presented us with the gift of another day." For the Communists would come at night.

Well, one night they came to Florina, and they beat on the doors and entered some of the houses. They came also to my mother's little house and beat on our door. But we were silent in the dark, only my mother prayed. And they did not come in. And my mother said, " God has saved us."

So my grandmother died and that was sad because she was a fine and good woman. But she was old. My mother grieved. " Now you are all that is left to me," she would say to me. " Sophia, you must never leave me."

I would never have left my mother but the order was given that the children should go away with the Red Cross to Oreocastro. That means in English " Beautiful Castle," and children from many villages in Macedonia were taken there so that they could be saved from the Communists. In many villages the guerrillas had taken the children away and hidden them in the mountains. I do not know why they took the children. Perhaps it was so that there would be no soldiers after a few years for Greece.

But my mother's heart broke when the order came for me to go to Oreocastro. She became sick and was in the hospital. And so I went away from Florina.

For a time it was very sad. All the children were lonely and we cried and we were afraid too. We had not a very easy time at first. We lived not in houses but in tents, and our food was beans and olives and bread. And after three months we had no shoes, and it grew cold. Every day there would be new children.

Then we would move when the Communists came to that place. Always there would be a careful watch and suddenly there would be word that we should move and we would all go. The Communists kept following.

We came to Salonika where there is the children's village. There were six hundred children there. And it was better because now we had a school and clothes, although not very many. We had kind teachers and learned to play games and we had songs to sing. It was better and some of the children forgot their homes, I think, but I could not forget.

There was a song we sang every night when the flag was lowered. These are the words in English:

> The day leaves.
> The night has come.
> In the mountains the heavy night falls.
> It is dark,
> But God protects us.
> Good night, sweet dreams.
> We have had a good time this day.
> Good night. Good night. Sweet dreams.

Is it not a nice song? But it made me cry, because I was lonely for my mother.

After she was in the hospital my mother tried to come to see me in Salonika, but she was on a bus, and it was destroyed by a mine in the road. My mother was hurt but I did not know until long afterwards. She was wounded and her mind was hurt.

Well, we had school at the children's village, and I was a good pupil as my father had wished, and I thought of him when I studied. And I did not expect that I would go to school after I finished the course. I knew about Anatolia College, but I was told that only the boys might win the scholarships. But it did not matter because I liked to study and I went on with my lessons anyway. Then suddenly one day it was announced that the girls might take the examination also. It was to be given in two weeks!

I can tell you that I studied those two weeks. I studied much history about Greece and Turkey before I was born, and hard mathematics, and other subjects. But I could not hope to pass the examination. Then I must write a composition, but what should I write about? I thought and thought and one night I dreamed about my village Florina. " I will write about Florina! " I said. " But not about the war and the Communists. I will write about my father playing on the organ, and about the mountains, and about my childhood." And that is what I wrote.

And then I won a scholarship! It was very wonderful, and I think it was because I wrote the composition. And now I am a scholar!

Well, you will want to know what a Greek schoolgirl of sixteen thinks about. I have thought of many things. I believe my thoughts are not the same as the thoughts of most of my friends. I do not know why that is, but it may be because I have been so much alone.

I have thought about going to study in America. And I should like to do that because I would like to bring much back from America to Greece. I would like to help Greek people to have better homes. I would like to help Greek children to have better schools, and more opportunities like mine to study and to be scholars. I would like to be a teacher in my country and I would like to be a teacher of Home Economics.

Well, I have thought about my mother and my father and my uncle and my grandmother. They are all dead except my mother, and she is sick in the hospital. But they were all good people, and I would like to think of all the good things they said that I can remember, and it will help me all my life. Yes, I believe that they are alive but I do not know how. I do not really believe in death, and I think this may be because I have seen it happen to so many people.

Yes, I think about the war. It is foolish to say, " Let us forget it," because it is here with us all the time. It is foolish to say, " We shall never have another one," because I think maybe we will have another one. But I do not believe in war any more than I believe in death. No, I do not hate the Germans or the Communists either. I do not hate anybody. I do not believe these people or any people are bad. I believe they are ignorant and wrong. I believe they need to be taught. But war does not teach anybody anything except sorrow and more war.

Yes, in a way I think I am happy. I have a great deal to do.

No. I am not different from other people, except that I have thought of a great many things by myself.

CHAPTER THREE

Democracy With a Greek Look

A girls' school — a Christmas bazaar — $2,000 — the life of a whole village saved! It sounds like an American success story. But it happened, and is still happening, in Greece.

The school is Pierce College, an American college for Greek girls at Elleniko, just outside Athens. The story is about students with vision, agencies which cooperated, people who could use help, and a miracle in the making.

It all began with the annual college bazaar last winter, when $2,000 were raised, and earmarked to help one of the thousand Greek villages demolished in the long succession of wars in Greece.

The girls went first to the Friends of the Villages organization, for advice about using their $2,000. Here they learned about Neochorakian, a little village in the mountains, about two hundred miles away. Neochorakian had been pillaged by the Italians in 1943, burned by the Germans in 1944, sacked and plundered again by Communist guerrillas in 1947, and twice evacuated. In 1950 the villagers had returned to the sites of their ruined homes to start over once more, with no money, no animals, no clothing, and not one whole building left to live in. The question for the college girls was not what to *do* with the large sum of $2,000, but how to *begin* — with only $2,000.

First, two of the girls and a faculty advisor made a weekend trip to Neochorakian, and tramped over the mountainside, visiting every one of the forty-two families of the village.

The people were trying. Already stone walls for most of the houses were rebuilt. But these still had no doors, or windows, or floors, and no furniture. Poverty was distressing. Most of the people were barefoot in the snow, and in rags. All were hungry.

Until midnight that Friday, the two girls sat up before the wee fireplace in the one-room house of the village president, discussing all these problems with Mr. Kitsos and other villagers who dropped in to talk. After the villagers went away the girls rolled themselves in blankets on the floor, and for the rest of the night they schemed and planned.

These people had no way of earning a living. Agriculture could no longer support them, as before. They needed new small industries, for earning cash money. But how could $2,000 start even one small industry?

The Sperchios river, which looked like a harmless trickle in dry weather, was a source of trouble because in flood time it covered the vast bottom land and destroyed whole plantings. To re-channel a river, or to build flood walls, if possible at all, would be expensive. Neochorakian couldn't do it. The girls couldn't either, with $2,000.

The villagers were proud of the newly built school house, but it needed outside toilets and drainage tiles for the backyard.

And they needed a church. The church is the center of the life of a Greek village, but theirs had been burned by the German army. Perhaps more than anything they needed a church.

Back in Elleniko the girls of the college tackled the overwhelming problem of providing industries, building sheds and toilets, damming a river and erecting a church — with $2,000. Such matters, they decided, required government and agency cooperation. They put their money in the bank, formed committees, and bravely carried their village to headquarters at Athens.

It was a project which kindled the imagination of officials and touched their hearts, and it was something new in old Greece to see young college girls eagerly planning constructive service for their own people. Everybody wanted to share in the job for Neochorakian.

CARE promised food parcels, the World Council of Churches sent clothing and blankets, Friends of the Villages offered shovels and picks and forks, the Save the Children Fund sent school supplies. Other agencies brought linens, cutlery, dishes, and buckets. The army promised trucks for transportation to the village.

All this — and $2,000 still in the bank!

While relief agencies gathered tangibles, the girls set about conferring with government committees about flood control, small industries and building projects, and the outcome of all this was another achievement — the first official public visitation out of Athens, to a village in southern Greece. This is what happened.

About the middle of February a team from the Agricultural Extension Division of the Economic Cooperation Administration, and the local representatives of the Greek Ministry of Agriculture, accompanied by a committee of college girls, went to Neochorakian to hold a town meeting, which was attended by heads of families (some of them women), for a discussion of village problems.

A town meeting! It harked back to Socrates' Athens.

A caravan of army trucks and jeeps lumbered over the hills from Athens, carrying the relief supplies, and also the makings of a feast. Village leaders and families, the school children and their teacher, visitors from nearby villages, officials from Athens, and of course those enterprising college girls —

all were there, joined in a common purpose. There was feasting, and there was singing and dancing, and there were eloquent speeches. But more than that — there was serious planning. Village leaders and technical advisors conferred together over problems and figured out solutions. Nothing like it had happened here before. The villagers declared that that day of the year would be an annual holiday for them forever.

Specifically the results of all this work are as exciting as the initial plans.

Flood control? The Ministry of Public Works is interested and has conferred with E.C.A. to see if funds may be secured to finance a project which will rescue the bottom land from the river, as well as the road above, which is one of the important mountain highways. They are considering a plan for a wire construction which will hold the rocks washed against the banks by the flood, and thus form a flood wall.

Industries? The Ministry of Agriculture will bring bee swarms if the village can provide hives. E.C.A. will sponsor a three months' " skill school " where village boys may learn carpentry and masonry, in order to build not only the bee hives, but the outhouses, the shed for school children to use in rainy weather, the windows and doors for houses.

Among the supplies provided by the relief agencies are ten looms, which can be used by the whole village as a nucleus for a small weaving industry. Cooperation of this kind has never been tried, but the villagers are convinced it can be done. The Ministry of Welfare will set up temporary quarters until a permanent one can be built by the men being trained in the skill school. The villagers have already laid the stone foundation. The hut is on its way.

The Ministry of Agriculture has sent fruit trees, and assisted in the planting of orchards.

Community cooperation has shown what it can do. Neochorakian wants to continue this plan of working together. The central building for the looms, and for the skill school, will be used also for a permanent community center, for more town meetings, for a library, for recreation, for sewing groups. The National Institute will furnish the center with books, and a radio, and sewing machines.

The church? The Archbishop at Athens is working with the villagers on this problem, and surely the new church will follow soon. Its site is ready on the hillside, just above the place where the old one stood before it was destroyed.

And the $2,000? Yes, some of it has been spent, with great care: $300 has been allocated to pay teachers for the three-month skill school; $100 will go to repair the looms; $40 will buy cement for the building projects; $175 was used for the feast on that day of the town meeting. The rest, the girls think, will be used to buy lambs and chickens. The plan is to provide each family with a female lamb, and to buy one male for the whole village.

More money will be needed, since the village project cannot be on its feet for two or three years more. But with a little money, much vision, planning and hard work, applied among a people who can use help to help themselves, there is no end to what can be done.

My own visit to the scene makes only a postscript to this modern miracle story. But after hearing all the facts, and meeting the college girls, I wanted to meet the other end of the story. I wanted to see for myself the kind of spirit that makes people who have suffered through nine years of war still able to take and use help constructively. And so, on a beautiful spring weekend, accompanied by a Greek staff member and two young people, I made the pilgrimage to Neochorakian.

The ride through the mountains was spectacular, up the slope of Parnes into the gorge of Giona, with the Marathon plains on our right and snow-crowned Parnassos on our left, and past the road leading to the Thermopylae pass, and finally descending from dizzy heights into the valley of that treacherous river Sperchios. From the time we reached the river we were greeted and welcomed from every stone cottage along the road. This, I was told, was Neochorakian, and they knew and welcomed us.

At the home of the village president, Mr. Kitsos, we were earnestly required to stay for dinner. One does not refuse the invitation of a president, even though one knows that there is not enough food in the house for guests. Sitting there in the tiny, bare, but immaculate whitewashed room, seeing the fine faces of the older people, and their handsome children, eating those fried potatoes, salad greens, bread and olives, I felt that no royal family in a palace could be more noble, and no palace more splendid. I recalled that the house had been rebuilt only recently, and that this one room represented a former two-story house, destroyed by guerrillas.

Standing outside the door a little later, I looked at the beauty of the spring planting of wheat, green all the way down to the Sperchios, and saw the apple trees provided by the Ministry of Agriculture. Looking on up the road I saw more neat tiny houses, far apart, and recently rebuilt. It was all serene and beautiful. I should never have guessed that less than two years before there had been nothing growing here, and nothing to see except war and destruction.

From a big rock in the schoolyard, sitting a little apart from the group, I watched the gathering of parents and children, called from all over the mountainside to meet us. I studied their faces, listened to their songs and saw their dancing, and enjoyed their frank delight over the simple gifts, the copy books and pencils and chocolate eggs which we had brought from the college. I marveled at how the youngsters who received the small pieces of chocolate rejoiced over seeing others receive large ones. I couldn't believe my eyes at finding no jealousy. Such instinctive generous joy in others' good fortune wasn't possible! But there it was, and I thought here must be one of the keys to this whole magic story. These people are not poor at all: they have no money, but they are rich in spirit.

I could see that the job of the Pierce College girls was not yet done. The conditions in Neochorakian were still distressing. There was still poverty, and there would be bitter cold in the coming winter, with homes that are not prepared for it. There were not enough clothes. There was not nearly enough money. But I began to see how it could and would be working out for those people. The leadership would come from the college girls. But what happened would come from the villagers themselves.

The climax of our visit was Mr. Kitsos's speech of appreciation, not merely for the gifts, as he said, but for all the help they had had, and for the fact that people cared. Even more he wished to express their gratitude, as Greek people, for the help that had come to Greece from America.

" In ancient Greece," he said (and it was interpreted to me), " Democracy was born, many centuries ago. But today it has had its rebirth in Greece, through the ministrations of America, the new Democracy."

On our way home, after many farewells and blessings, and along all the long beautiful way we had come, I thought about Mr. Kitsos, and Neochorakian, and Democracy.

Certainly, as this man suggested, the widening circles of action set in motion in Neochorakian by the girls at Pierce College represent a practical demonstration of the kind of

Democracy we like to call American, and in this sense America has " sent Democracy back to the Greeks."

But I believe we have among these young Greek girls, and in this proud village, a demonstration of Democracy with a new look — a modern young Greek look — that has lessons which should come back again to America.

I think perhaps the Pierce College girls have done a bigger job even than saving the life of a village.

CHAPTER FOUR

Easter in Lamia

The breathtaking three days of Easter in Lamia were ones I shall want always to remember. For weeks after, my mind was filled with warm colorful memories of little children running alongside our car, tossing flowers to us and crying, " Ya sas, ya sas! " (" Be Healthy! "), bells ringing madly in church towers, processions of lighted candles, the smell of incense, the lights from flares, the popping of firecrackers; and on Easter Sunday the sight of lambs roasting over spits in every backyard along the road, the cries of " Christos aneste! " (" Christ is risen! ") and the answer coming in a chorus from the Greeks in our car, " Alithos aneste! " (" Yes, certainly he is risen! ")

It was Mrs. Haniatou who persuaded me to include a story that would tell something about the religion of Greece.

" You must learn all that you can about our Greek Orthodox Church," she declared, " not because it is so good or so unique, but because without the Church there could not be Greece."

Mrs. Haniatou admitted frankly that she was not especially religious herself, but she was punctilious about keeping all the fast days because, as she said, " Following these customs is a part of being Greek. And it is not so much the religion that is important. Not many Greeks except the priests know what the religion is about. But the Church *is* Greece and Greece *is* the Church."

So it was arranged for me to make the trip in the Pierce College car to Lamia for Easter. In the party was Jim, a Greek who spoke an odd mixture of Greek and English. He was wearing an old army officer's uniform. There was Mrs. Haniatou, with a fancy red bandana tied around her head. There was her son Athanasios, a student attending Athens College. (Athanasios is seventeen, and his mother told me he had never had a home, because he had never been alive in a time when there was not war in Greece.) There was Philomela, a lovely Greek girl who spoke little, but whose intense dark eyes told eloquently of grief. She had lost her whole family, and most recently a brother very dear to her. And finally there was a beautiful and interesting Canadian girl who wore a bright striped skirt.

Early Friday morning we were all packed in the car with enough *tsoureki* (Easter bread baked with a red egg in the dough) and cheese and halvah and olives to last the weekend. We shook hands all around with the crowd of staff people who gathered at the kitchen door to wish us a safe journey, and went on our way with as warm a send-off as if we had planned to be gone for six months.

It was thrilling on that clear blue morning to start off toward the hills ahead, beyond which higher hills loomed, snow-capped. We seemed to be moving toward a great canvas painted on the horizon, and at the same time to be a part of another canvas, with blue sea on one side, and on the other white shining cottages, and green grass, and brilliant flowers.

While I was spellbound and quiet, trying to photograph in my memory the dazzling loveliness of the picture we were moving through, Mrs. Haniatou and Jim and Athanasios began singing ballads. I wished then for some kind of recording memory that would hold in my ears the lovely, graceful notes that no bird could have sung more sweetly. Most of the songs were funny, but they sounded sad to me. Mrs. Hani-atou, wiping her eyes, and choking with laughter, said, "Americans can afford to be sad over romantic trifles, but the Greeks carry even tragedy gaily. We must be gay or we would be dead."

Because the Greek Easter begins on Friday morning and lasts through the following Monday, this was a holiday; and in every village we could see preparations going on. There were hundreds of lambs lying in dead wooly heaps, waiting to be sold for the Sunday cooking. The markets were filled with red-dyed eggs, and windows were crowded with *tsoureki* and raisin bread, made only at Easter time. There was a Sabbath holiday air, not quiet — because the Greeks are never quiet — but festive. Every village square was filled with men dressed in their best, walking up and down together or sitting in the outdoor cafes, talking fast and furiously, perhaps about war and politics, or more likely about the weather. In Greece every subject is dealt with violently.

At lunch time we stopped in a little village and spread out our provisions on a bridge overlooking a magnificent water-fall that dropped straight off the mountain side. It was a beautiful spot, so neatly combed and brushed and white-washed for Easter that I was shocked to realize suddenly there on the bridge how close we were to the stark ruins of stone buildings. They were all around us and on up the narrow road above and down other roads below. I kept seeing more and more heaps of shattered buildings, some of them disguised with climbing green vines, some hidden by piles of stones stacked neatly in front so that the ruins hardly showed. But it was clear that not one building in that little village had escaped damage.

This was so in every village we rode through. I learned that most of the small whitewashed buildings we saw had been built or rebuilt during the past two years. All this had been accomplished by people so poor that even now they do not have enough to eat, or to wear.

The gaiety of the holiday was in startling contrast. I asked Mrs. Haniatou if Easter had been celebrated in this way during the various military occupations. She said that Easter had never been without celebration, although sometimes it was mostly in their hearts, and only the last two Easters had been really gay ones.

The last stretch of road into Lamia was the most spectacular I have ever seen. We had been climbing most of our way up and up into the hills until our road lay among those snow caps we had looked at from farther below. Now from a dizzy height and dimly through clouds, we could see our village far away beneath us. It seemed practically at our feet, yet so small that we might have picked it up in one hand.

The road wound down like a worm around the mountain, with terrifying hairpin twists, which we could see and dread long before we came to them — mile after mile of turning and winding, sometimes with the village showing beneath us, growing gradually larger and clearer. At last we could distinguish houses and streets, and could see the spire of the cathedral in the center. When we finally arrived, we felt as if we had known Lamia from its childhood and had watched it grow into a large-sized town.

We found rooms in a small plain hotel located on the village square with the suggestive name " Aeneas," and about ten o'clock that night we went over to the cathedral. Already the square was sparkling with candles and everybody carried armloads of unlighted ones. As they were being sold in the entrance of the cathedral, I bought one for a thousand drachmas (which is about six cents) and stuck it in one of the brass holders as the other people were doing — but not, I'm sure, with the proper meditations that go along with lighting candles in a church. I confess that most of my mind was at work figuring out how great sacrifices those poor people had made of things they needed in order to buy their armloads of candles, and how much money was being spent in that cathedral. After the candle lighting I took one of the straight-up-and-down seats along the side of the wall, and settled down for the rest of the night with Mrs. Haniatou next to me, interpreting and answering questions.

The cathedral was like the usual Greek Orthodox church, but more elaborate, with life-sized pictures of the apostles painted on the doors at the front facing us. Before the doors of the apostles was a large open square, with high pulpits for the " singers " on either side. In the center of the open square was the " tomb of Christ," a box-like structure with all four sides open, and a flower-covered dome for a top. Mrs. Haniatou told me that the women and children begin on the evening of the day before Good Friday to cover the " tomb " with flowers and work on it all night.

There was a big crowd around the tomb, so that we had to push through and then stand in line to see the inside of it, where a picture done in silver and a silver Bible lay on the floor. Mrs. Haniatou explained that these represented the " body of Christ." All the people who passed in line kissed both the picture and the book, crossed themselves, and then walked on.

The marching past the tomb continued for about an hour, while two " singers " read and chanted back and forth, and others from the audience, all men and boys, joined them, so that there was a lovely harmony of choral speaking and chanting.

During all this time more and more people continued to crowd into the church, lighting candles, until it was one great

blaze of light. At a certain point in the reading about twenty
soldiers marched down the center aisle, stood in line before
the tomb, removed their helmets in unison, and then took posi-
tions as guards about it. At another point in the reading the
whole congregation began to sing with the leaders, while
eight girls, dressed in black and carrying baskets of flowers,
tossed blossoms onto the " body of Christ."

A few minutes before midnight Mrs. Haniatou passed the
word around among us that it was time to leave. We pushed
through the crowd in the church, and the crowd outside, and
hurried over to the hotel to sit in our balcony windows overlooking the square.

At midnight the bell began to toll, the people in the square
below, all carrying lighted candles, parted, and the sea of
candles divided like the Red Sea into two banks of light on
either side of the center of the square. Then a band playing
a funeral march came out through the church doors. Behind
the band, marching in time to the slow funeral music, came
four little choir boys in white robes, carrying icons on poles.
One carried a cross covered all over with flowers. Behind the
boys marched four priests in robes of blue, red and gold, and
carrying scrolls. Then came the " tomb " borne aloft on
the shoulders of six army men. After them came the girls
with the flower baskets, and after them the mass of people
surged out of the church, all with their lighted candles. They
moved into the center of the square, looking like a fiery river
flowing between two walls of fire on either side.

Just at the center of the square they all stopped. The priests
alternately chanted and sang, although we could barely hear
them through the hum and rumble from the crowd of people,
and the occasional popping of firecrackers. After the little
ceremony the band struck up its slow tune again, the soldiers
lifted the tomb to their shoulders, and they all marched on

through the square, the crowd pressing behind them, and on up the hill.

This procession was scarcely off the square when we heard music from the other side, and down another street came a second procession from another church, carrying another " tomb." They too had a band and priests and flower girls, and crowds of people following with lighted candles. This line marched under our windows while the crowd in the square moved over to meet it. While the second procession paused in the center for its ceremony, still another appeared. Four others followed, so close together that every street on the square was filled with moving masses of lights, some coming in, some going out, some stopping in the center. In every direction as far as we could see there were lights, and the square itself was one sea of lights. And all the while the cathedral bell tolled, and the bands played the funeral music.

We waited on our balcony spellbound, until the last procession had wound its way up the hill leaving only a few scattered sparkling lights below us in the square.

In the few moments before we fell wearily to sleep in our beds at the Aeneas, Mrs. Haniatou repeated to me some of the lessons I should learn from all this. " It is the burial you have seen," she said. " The burial of Christ. And next you will see the ' Resurrection.' The ' Resurrection ' is a little different. It is like and not like the burial. It is the greatest experience a Greek can know."

The " Resurrection " was to take place in most Greek village churches at midnight on Saturday, but in the Lamia cathedral it would be celebrated at dawn Sunday.

Saturday was another holiday, festive without being quiet. In some ways Saturday reminded me of our pre-Christmas shopping days, with the throngs of people in the streets and markets making last-minute purchases of candles, Easter bread, and food to follow the fast. There was a feeling of anticipation, joyous waiting for something wonderful to happen, which made me very curious to know about this " Resurrection " I was presently to see.

Four o'clock on Sunday morning seemed pretty early, but in the end we did get up for the celebration, and we went at two o'clock instead of four because Mrs. Haniatou said that, if we were going at all, we ought to be on time.

But even at two the bell was tolling at gloomy intervals. There was some light in the sanctuary, and a good deal of activity going on behind the painted doors in the front. Women were not allowed back there, Mrs. Haniatou told me, but in occasional glimpses we had when the doors swung open, we could see the choir boys putting on their white robes, and the priests getting fixed up in their costumes. It was like peeping behind the curtain before the play begins.

I liked watching the early morning gathering, and seeing the people come up the aisle carrying loaves of bread wrapped in napkins, and small bottles of olive oil. The choir boys met them at the painted doors, received the offerings, returned the emptied bottles, and then shut the doors again. I marveled at the look of peace on the faces of those worshippers after they had delivered their gifts, and were walking back up the aisle with their empty bottles.

The service in the church was much like the one on Friday night, as Mrs. Haniatou had said, with even the tomb back in its old place, and always the bells in the tower were tolling. But there was something peaceful and quiet and good about it that was truly different. It was a time and an occasion for worship.

Shortly before four o'clock Mrs. Haniatou whispered the signal to go, and we followed her out into the square again, a quiet, chilly square contrasted with the festival of lights on

Friday. A little platform had appeared there in the meantime, in the center. This, I understood, was the stage of the
" Resurrection."

After just a few moments the procession came out of the
church, choir boys, cross and icons, the four priests and the
guard of soldiers carrying their guns. It seemed incongruous to me always to see the army guard, but Mrs. Haniatou
reminded me that the Greek church and the army are almost
one and the same.

The soldiers stood in a line all around the platform, while
the four priests took turns reading from the scrolls and chanting, joined by some of the men and boys who stood round
about. The bells continued to toll.

I was interested in watching the audience, especially the
weary children, six and seven and eight, who stood, wide-
eyed with wonder, half-awed, half-terrified and wholly fas-
cinated. Everyone was quiet.

Suddenly there was a little wave of anticipation through
the crowd, the bells stopped ringing, the priest paused in the
reading, and there was one electric moment of silence. Then
the priest cried out, as if he'd just heard the news, " Christos
aneste! " (" Christ is risen! ")

And what a response! The soldiers raised their guns and
crashed them to the ground, firecrackers burst and boomed
on every side, Roman candles whooshed through the air, the
people laughed and cried and cracked their red eggs together
and shook hands. The bells began again, no longer tolling,
but ringing in double-quick time. And the whole crowd
began to sing together the Easter hymn.

It was a stunning moment. Tears came into my eyes in
spite of the effort to be nonchalant. It was heartbreaking
somehow to see a people so poor, who had suffered and lost
so much and who might never in all their lives be secure in

anything except in their own stout hearts, laugh and cry with joy in such abandon. I kept wondering if they would have another " Resurrection " to enjoy.

Next morning we started back on the long beautiful road from Lamia, and all the way we waved to the families sitting by their roasting lambs in the backyards. They waved to us, and gave us the greeting, " Christ is risen! " and our Greeks answered back, " He is indeed risen! " It was very beautiful and kindly and full of friendship. Perhaps the joyousness of the day was especially keen and deep because for so long there had been no celebration " except in the heart."

That evening in my room I recalled what Mrs. Haniatou had said.

" Do you not see that every candle is burned for the Greek hearts that were broken, for the Greek homes that were destroyed, for the Greek children who were carried away from their land, and for the Greek spirit which not any of these losses could destroy? Do you not know that when ' the body of Christ ' was raised in the ceremony, and when the priest shouted ' Christos aneste,' it was that Greece could see the dawning of the day? Is it not clear to you that in the resurrection scene the men and women and children of Greece take heart, and once again begin to build? There would be no villages for you to see rising again if it had not been for the unity we have in the Church! "

FROM THE MIDDLE EAST

CHAPTER FIVE

The Arabs and the Jews

The trouble between the Arabs and the Jews is centered in a patch of land about as large as the state of Vermont, mostly desert — but the trouble involves 40,000,000 Arabs in outlying nations, 350,000,000 non-Arab Moslems in other countries, and Jews all over the world.

Although we must not become too deeply involved in political issues, yet in order to understand the people caught in the midst of this problem, we must try to get some historical facts straight. Here, briefly, is the situation.

For many centuries Arabs and Jews have been living in Palestine together, people of the same racial stock, but divided by religion. After the destruction of Jerusalem in the year 70 A.D. the Jewish people were scattered throughout Europe; later they migrated to America, and some went far into Asia. In most places they continued to live a separate existence, based primarily upon their unique religious convictions. In many countries they have been discriminated against and often bitterly persecuted. We all know the tragic story of their sufferings in Germany before and during the second world war.

Out of this separateness, as well as the discrimination, grew the idea of a return to Palestine, the ancient home of the Jews, and later the idea of reestablishment of the Jewish nation. Palestine, however, was also the ancient home of the Arabs, and for centuries many more Arabs than Jews lived there.

The " return " of the Jews began as long as sixty-five years ago, with legal purchases of land from Arab owners, and the development of it by Jewish immigrants. In this way settlement by Jews increased slowly year after year.

After World War I, Palestine was placed under British mandate. The idea of a Jewish homeland in Palestine was brought up in Parliament, and plans were widely publicized and discussed. These plans were bitterly opposed by the Arabs. In 1947 Britain brought the Arab-Jewish problem to the United Nations, and a plan of partition was worked out which gave to the Jews a large portion of Palestine, to be a Jewish nation, Israel, on land most of which was then owned by Arab people.

The Arabs then had a choice between two courses of action. They could accept the United Nations decision; this meant that those Arabs whose property was included in the prospective Israeli nation could become citizens of Israel — which to the Arabs meant being subject to an alien people. Or they could refuse to accept the plan of partition, and could fight.

The Arabs chose to fight.

When the British withdrew from Palestine in 1948, open warfare between the Arabs and Jews broke out (May, 1948). A year later, a cease-fire was arranged by the United Nations (May, 1949). By this time the Jews had occupied more land than the U.N. partition plan included. During and since the end of the war there has been a vast movement of Arab refugees out of the Jewish state, and a vast moving in of Jewish refugees and immigrants from Europe, Iran, Iraq, and Yemen, as well as from other parts of the world, to fill up the space left vacant by the fleeing Arabs. The Jews say that the Arab refugees left their homes voluntarily. The Arabs say they either were forced out or were frightened away.

There are now only about 170,000 Arabs left in the portion of Palestine called Israel. Of these, over 20,000 * are refugees who a few years ago lived comfortably in their homes there, but who are now homeless and in temporary quarters. There are more than 850,000 other displaced Arabs camping in Syria, Lebanon, Jordan, and the Gaza strip west of Israel. The Gaza strip is now under Egyptian military control.

The United Nations Relief and Works Agency to Palestine Refugees has been feeding (inadequately) and housing (in tents, barracks and mud huts) these homeless Arabs for four years, while the best minds in the world have tried to find a solution which will satisfy both Arabs and Jews. The Blandford plan, or the " $250,000,000 integration plan " as it is sometimes called, is now being considered. Simply put, this means that new homes for the refugees would be purchased in neighboring Arab states which have room for them. The refugees would be moved from their present temporary quarters to these designated places, and the development of new cities and towns and agricultural and industrial expansion would be financed by the United Nations until the Arabs are able to support themselves. This is a long way from the repatriation which the refugees want. But the plan includes a clause indicating that acceptance of " integration " on these terms may be considered a temporary measure, and does not preclude the right of the Arabs to reoccupy their old homes, or to receive restitution for their losses, if and when this is or may be possible.

The Arab refugees frankly oppose the plan because they believe acceptance of it would preclude repatriation, regardless of the palliative clause. They want their homes — as they consider them — and they want them now. The govern-

* All statistics in this section are given in round numbers and drawn from the Blandford report to the seventh session of the General Assembly of the United Nations, June 30, 1952.

ments which have room to receive them (mainly Syria) object to the plan because it would make the nation Israel an accepted *fait accompli*, and, once Israel is officially entrenched in Palestine, they believe it will insist upon continuing expansion and further occupation of Arab-held lands. And so, while the conferences and the arguments go on and on, the homeless people continue to be homeless.

At the same time there are in Israel more than 650,000 newcomers since 1948, Jews from nearly every country of the world. These are not all refugees, nor have they all come from countries where they have been discriminated against. Many have come at the call of the Zionists who see in the establishment of this nation the fulfillment of Biblical prophecy. Many have come because they thought they would be better off in a Jewish state than in a country where their religion set them apart from other people. A great many have come because they had lost their homes in Europe during World War II. Others have come from that part of Palestine left to the Arabs after the Palestinian war, or from Iraq and Yemen, where they are not welcome among a largely Moslem population.

When you consider how small Palestine is as a whole, and how very small is the part called Israel, you can have some idea of the overcrowded situation created by these large migrations into the territory.

At present there exists an uneasy truce between Israel and Arab Palestine. Israel fears that the Arabs may attempt to regain the land captured in the war by the Jews, and the Arabs fear that overcrowded Israel will try to take more territory than she now occupies. These fears prevail especially in the city of Jerusalem — which is now divided between the two enemies, with the Jews occupying the modern part of the city, and the Arabs the old part. In this small, old section of Jerusalem are crowded most of the Arabs who formerly owned large houses in the new part of the city. Their former homes are now occupied by the Jews who have come in.

Our thought, in presenting stories from the Middle East, is not to try to stir up partisan feelings. It is, rather, that all of us may remember that at the bottom of every international or political impasse and resolution there are human beings who live and work and love and suffer, and whose whole lives may be affected by these situations.

Our hope is that a new generation may study to be wiser, less selfish, less fearful, more understanding than our own, and that diplomacy will come to be understood in terms of individual people.

CHAPTER SIX

Round About Damascus

In considering a visit to the Arab countries of the Middle East, I hoped that I might know a few at least of the million or more homeless people who had left that part of Palestine which is now Israel. I wanted to talk with them, if it were possible, not as an official, nor as a representative from any organization, but as another human being. I was not sure that it could be done. But when I discussed this with Mr. George Barakat, Executive Director of the American Middle East Relief, he thought it was entirely possible and a good idea.

It was therefore with the help of the American Middle East Relief, as well as the Egyptian government through its embassy at Washington and the United Nations Relief and Works Agency to Palestine Refugees, that I was able to visit Arab refugee camps in Lebanon, Jordan, Syria, and Gaza. As I met these people and talked with them in the tents on the desert and in barracks and mosques and crowded city quarters, I was reminded often of what Mr. Barakat had said to me before I left New York:

"Very few people understand the Arabs. We need someone to bring to the west a first-hand report of this kind from the people in the refugee camps. You will be shocked by what you will see, but you may be surprised and challenged by the spirit you will find still living among an old, old people. When you talk with the Arab refugees, try to remember that these people have been homeless and hungry for four years. Try to face with them another winter in the tents. No — it will not be a happy experience. But please try to understand the Arabs."

Damascus is the capital of Syria, the seat of the Syrian university, and one of the oldest cities in the world. Paul met Ananias there after he had had his strange experience on the road from Jerusalem. The Damascus bazaars are famous. The U.S. Consulate there and the Egyptian Embassy and some other buildings are impressive. There is a good and famous hotel. There are some quite luxurious dwelling places. There are mosques, and there are many many tourists.

There are also about 84,000 destitute refugees camping in mosques, schoolhouses, and tents in and around Damascus. These are the responsibility just now of UNRWA and the Syrian government working through PARI (Palestinian Arab Refugee Institution).

My visit to the refugee camps of Damascus was in charge of Mr. Abou Dourrah, who is the cultural attaché of the Egyptian Legation in Syria. Even knowing ahead of time how these things are arranged, I was a little disconcerted when Mr. Abou Dourrah arrived with not one, but two carloads of officials, impressive in tarboush and uniform, and two newspaper reporters to interview the party before it started.

The group included a U.N. social worker, Miss Mary Souda, who had studied at London University, and seemed a friendly and approachable person. The rest of the officials were representatives of PARI, the Egyptian Legation, the United Nations, or from the local administration at Damascus. We must have made quite a procession, speeding through the oldest town in the world in automobiles, and far too impressive to the refugees in the tents. But that was the way we went.

From the busy city of Damascus our party sped across several miles of desert, gleaming white in the sun, and stopped before the crumbling walls of an ancient hostelry. Just inside the great open gateway a few ragged children gathered to look at us, but without much interest. Several men, sitting or lying in spots around the big courtyard where the wall offered shelter from the wind, opened their eyes, raised their heads, and then dropped off to sleep again. A caravan of camels today might have attracted more attention than the two automobiles.

" Is it not significant," asked Miss Souda, " that the inn which once sheltered pilgrims on their way to the holy place, today shelters pilgrims waiting to return to their homeland? " She herself is a refugee from Haifa.

" But these pilgrims are sheltered in stables," she went on. " Here are the places where camels and donkeys used to sleep. Now human beings sleep in them. Is there something in your religion about a baby born in a stable? "

We walked then across the courtyard toward an entrance in the wall which gaped dark ahead of us. There was no one at the door — if it was a door — and we went on through and down a circular stone stair, so dark that I had to feel my way along to keep from falling over the rough steps.

" A camel couldn't have walked down these steps! " I called back to Miss Souda, who was just behind me.

" This is the cellar where the food was kept," she told me. " You will get to the bottom presently."

At the bottom I stopped again, and waited for my eyes to grow used to the darkness. There was a sort of stall on one side, and at first it appeared to be empty. Then there was a sound of water splashing, and a voice at my elbow startled me. Gradually I could distinguish the form of a woman, and half by seeing and half by hearing reckoned that she must be washing something in a tub. Beyond her on the floor was a dark heap, and a slight moan indicated that the heap was a small person, a child perhaps, lying under a blanket.

" It is her son. He is sick," Miss Souda said in my ear. It was reassuring to have her there close behind me. The others had stayed up in the courtyard because there was not enough room for them below.

" Go in the room if you like," said Miss Souda. " The child is not asleep."

But in some embarrassment at having barged into a sick-room, I turned from the entranceway, and almost fell into another stall on the other side. This was a little lighter because of a narrow slit in the heavy stone wall where it reached above the ground. A woman stood back in a corner. There was a mat on the floor, and four gaudy paper pictures pasted on the wall opposite the window slit.

The woman was saying something. Miss Souda translated. " She says, ' Please, can't you get us out of here? ' "

Miss Souda spoke to the woman in Arabic, and they talked for a moment.

" I have told her that you are an American, and that you are here to learn of the sufferings of the homeless," Miss Souda told me. " She asks Allah to protect you. And she wants you to know that this is not the way she is accustomed to living. She is ashamed. Her husband was a farmer in north Palestine, and they were not rich but they were clean. She is ashamed to be in a filthy place."

I came up out of that dark hole feeling bleak. Mr. Abou Dourrah noted my expression and said he understood that horses lived better in the state of Kentucky than these people.

Our next stop was at a town settlement just a short distance from the end of " the Street called Straight," where Paul met Ananias and told him about his strange experience on the road.

In the old days there had been a large Jewish school in the great building surrounding a large courtyard. Today Arab families live in the building, as well as in tents covering a large vacant lot on the other side of the road. The courtyard is used as a playground for the three hundred children. Only the top floor of the building is used for schoolrooms.

We went along the corridors of the lower floors, passing several of the " homes." As in the Mosque barracks the partitions for family cells were made of blankets or pieces of ragged cloth strung up short distances apart.

Some of them had small windows, some none at all. Beds were grass mats laid on the floor at night and folded up during the day. Some of the families had tiny kerosene single-burner stoves for cooking, and a few pans. There were no chairs. Some of the more fortunate had managed to bring a few of their own possessions, but most of these they had sold for food, Miss Souda told me. In one enclosure there hung, as a partition, a beautiful oriental carpet, one treasure kept from what must have been a luxurious home.

" These people were not farmers like the others," Miss Souda told me. " They were rich people with fine houses, and they had not only the simple things, but they had the luxuries as well. Can you think of the difference — one day a house, ten great beautiful rooms, furniture and clothing! The next — this! Can you think, suddenly to have no *bathroom!* And no food at all! "

They received flour, rice, margarine and very little else from the UNRWA — a total of 1600 calories per person per day. In some families where the men could find small jobs in Damascus they could have some extras. Many of the children went about town running errands to earn a few piastres, and a few had taken to begging.

Miss Souda urged me to go into each cubicle and to look closely at the life there. In one of them, while the family stood by, she went about pointing at the rags, the mats, the poor little kerosene stove, the sticks of furniture sent by kind people in Damascus.

" This is the way they live," she exclaimed, taking in the whole barren enclosure with a gesture that included the woman and the two children clinging to her ragged skirts.

I backed out hastily, protesting. " It isn't fair to disturb their privacy and to look into their homes this way."

" Homes? " she exclaimed. " These are not their homes! Their homes are decent places — on the other side! " Then she added, " If you lived here would you call it your home? "

That was all, but she made me feel personally responsible for all the miseries of the Arabs.

After walking through the " homes " on the lower floors, we climbed up to the schoolrooms. These were rooms opening on a balcony overlooking the courtyard where on one side the boys were playing, and on the other the girls. In the class-rooms other groups were having classes. All the doors were open, and we could hear the children, in one room chanting the Koran, in another the Arabic lesson, in another arithmetic, which they learned from the abacus.

In these classrooms rows of children sat crowded together on benches, some with desks, some without. The boys had close-cropped hair, so that standing in the doorway one looked down on rows and rows of round black heads. Most of them wore blue coats and short pants, and the girls had black or brown dresses. When our party entered, the youngsters sprang from their seats and extended their right arms with forefinger pointed toward us in greeting.

At the door to the first room, the PARI official turned to me.

" Well, now we have brought you at last to children. You asked to see children. Here are children. Do with them as you wish."

I was at a loss to know what to do, with two carloads of officials and three school staff people standing by, and sixty interested and curious little boys staring straight at me. It was a problem. I hesitated while they all waited expectantly. Finally I suggested that the PARI official ask the children any questions he wanted which would give me an idea of what they were thinking about, and permit Miss Souda to interpret questions and answers. These came like an exchange of gun shots, so quickly that she could hardly keep up.

" Where are your homes? "

Most of them said Haifa and Jaffa.

" Why did you leave them? "

" We were driven away! "

" Who drove you away? "

" The Jews."

" Who are your friends? "

" We have no friends."

" Who are your enemies? "

" Everybody."

" What are you going to do when you grow up? "

" Fight the Jews."

" What do you want most? "

" We want to go home."

Even the small ones chorused the answers without any great emotion, and as if they stated facts which had got fixed firmly in their minds long before, settled facts that would not change. Some of them raised their hands and told their own stories briefly, cheerfully even, so that only the words were horrible.

" My father was killed. My mother died. We had a house with five rooms. I alone stay."

As we went on to other rooms the PARI official asked the same questions, and every time the chorus became more sickeningly familiar.

" For whom is Palestine? "

" Ours, ours, ours! "

" Who are your enemies? "

I couldn't miss it, even in Arabic, and they counted us off on their thin brown fingers. " L'Inglise, l'American! — Yehud! " *Yehud* came last.

" When the Americans send you food, clothing and money, how can you say they are not friends? "

" They send us alms. We do not want alms. Once we gave them. Now we must ourselves be beggars! "

" But why do you say the Americans are your enemies? "

" They let the Jews take our homes."

" Aren't you in your homes now? "

" Our homes are in Palestine! "

I left that room feeling sick, and out on the balcony we were served with Turkish coffee in tiny cups. Down in the courtyard below, the other groups of boys and girls were playing marching games. The girls especially looked very pretty in the march, all with black dresses and red bows tied in their hair.

Our party talked among themselves in Arabic, and it was a relief to be left alone to drink the coffee and watch the children in the court — and think. Only Miss Souda waited near me for some comment. Finally I gathered up courage and asked her directly:

" Have the children been taught to make these answers? They speak too quickly. Is this a put-up job? "

She hesitated.

" I see what you mean," she answered me, slowly. " They seem glib. But it is not a ' put-up job,' as you say. They have been taught in a way. But it is by their wrongs they were taught. They having nothing else to think about, to talk about, to dream about. When they are sleeping they dream of their homes and their gardens. When they are eating and playing they talk of going back home. They have taught themselves."

"But this bitterness they have against us — has it always been this way?" I asked.

"Certainly not!" she exclaimed vehemently. "Who should know better than I how deeply we in Palestine have respected your people? Your missionaries, your social workers, even your tourists we respect, and we are grateful to them, every one! But it is that now we are helpless, and when we look to your nation for support, nothing happens! Nothing except another winter without homes for our people!"

When we reached the court just below us, the boys were having a physical-education hour, and as we passed them on our way out to the street they stood at attention in six straight lines facing us, and sang a song in Arabic. It sounded like a war song. When Miss Souda translated the words the song went something like this:

> We are the children who lost our homes in Palestine!
> Our pride was broken; our hearts were broken.
> Our homes and our lands were laid in ashes.
> We shall grow into men to destroy our enemies.
> We shall return to our homes.

Miss Souda looked at me curiously, and again waited for me to comment. Finally she said, "You are thinking about the children; there is no necessity for you to speak."

"I am thinking about the children," I agreed.

"Tonight," she went on with understanding, "tonight I am afraid you will hear them when you try to sleep." She smiled a little wearily. "I hear them. All through the cold winter I have heard them. And I know they will be cold — and sick for home."

"I know they will be cold — and homesick," I repeated.

In the hotel dining room that evening there were seven

Americans at the table next to mine, ordering Scotch and bourbon, and making a disturbance because the liquor was flat and coffee wasn't served with the meal. The waiter was upset, and when I pushed back my plate he said rather testily, " You don't like? "

" No," I said, " I don't like."

CHAPTER SEVEN

How Many Miles to Bethlehem?

Bethlehem is such a pretty little town! It has the sort of timeless dignity that would make it a fitting birthplace for any king. And if there were angels — real angels — it is more than likely they were hovering that night over Bethlehem. If one should sit on a hillside above the town, with the big night stretching around him, he would no doubt see a star almost any time.

What is not fitting at all is that outside the town, and not very far away, there should be a ragged tent town huddling close to a hill, in an undignified way, mocking Christian history, mocking Christianity itself. One of the sad facts about misery and squalor is that they have no dignity.

I came to Bethlehem, wondering how it would be to see the town apart from its ancient symbolism.

It kept its Sabbath atmosphere even in pouring rain. Although the time was long past Christmas and not late enough for Easter (these are the seasons when tourist business is brisk in the Holy Land), there was a party from America in town, about fifty of them, and things were humming. The doors of all the little shops were wide open in the rain.

Josef Haddad, the camp director there, belongs to the twentieth century and is an old friend. He has a wide open smile, a round Irish-looking face and freckles, and I have never seen him when he wasn't wearing khaki trousers and a sweat shirt. He is rather like an American college boy (which he expects to be next year). While swapping slang with him, I could almost forget that Josef was a veteran of the Arab-Jewish war, fought on the walls of Jerusalem, and had a miraculous escape from death. Through a shrewd sort of underground trick which would equal any sort of adventure story we could pull out of the story books, he was rescued by the girl who is now his fiancée. If this were a war story it would be a pleasure to write about Josef's adventures. But this book has to do with what follows war.

We stood for a few minutes on the hill above the Church of the Nativity, watching the people go in and come out.

" Bethlehem is lovely even in the rain," I said. " One could stay here for a long time, I think."

He smiled but did not look convinced.

" You know, most Americans say that," he said. " But they seldom stay. And while they're here they don't see the real town — only the churches and the bazaars."

I remarked that we'd picked a bad day to go to the refugee camps, but he said cheerfully that it was an ideal day for that purpose. He was very glad we hadn't waited for the rainy season to be ended.

" When spring comes and the little flowers bloom all over the hills, and the wind blows a melody instead of a bedlam, the refugees' problem looks like Boy Scout camping. But it's no fun to live in a tent, especially a piece of a tent in winter," he said.

He turned from the direction of the town a little reluctantly. " Well — this isn't seeing the tents," he said. " Let's get going."

Out in the cold and rain and mud we went then, to climb into a jeep and bump along toward the camp, over ruts and furrows. By this time it was pouring, and with rubbers and a raincoat on I felt like — well, like an American, which is not the best way to feel among people who have not enough clothes to cover their backs.

We went into tent after tent, each of which seemed worse than the one before it. Many had been completely destroyed during the recent storms. All had been damaged, and the relentless rain poured in through gaping holes and ran in little rivers underneath the canvas sides. Every time a front flap was raised I stooped down and looked into darkness that gradually lightened to show the holes overhead and the rain pouring in and the people huddled together into the drier spots, crouching by little piles of charcoal that only filled the darkness with smoke and gave no heat at all.

" They creep about in an effort to run away from the wetness," Josef observed.

Some had pieces of sacking or torn army blankets spread on the ground to sleep on at night and sit on during the day. Most of the men and women and all the children were barefoot, cold, sick, dirty. One wondered if these could be human beings. How could human beings possibly stay alive in such conditions?

But they were human all right. As we left each tent they came out and crowded around us, gesticulating, shouting in Arabic which Josef translated for me.

" Tell the Americans how we live! " they were saying. " Tell the rich Americans what suffering is. Tell them about the homes we left. Tell them we want our homes! "

In front of one tent a young man, probably twenty-five although he looked much older, stopped us, reached down and picked up a tiny boy who was clinging to his knees. The baby was a beauty, blonde, blue-eyed, quiet. His father held him out to me, the child smiled, and as I made a motion to speak to him, the father snatched him back, and shouted to me in Arabic.

Josef hesitated this time before he translated.

" He says, ' This little child shall be taught that all the world are his enemies, and his children shall remember, and his children's children, the miseries of the Arab people. And they will never forget. For I promise you that we shall not die, I and my son and my son's sons. Weak in body, strong in spirit, we shall live to remember, and to curse our betrayers, the British and the Americans! ' "

Josef tried to modify this.

" They do not understand what they are saying," he explained. " The man is not angry at you or at the English or the Americans. He is really angry at the cold, and the holes in the tent. You must try to understand how they feel — that they are cold and hungry."

Then the baby screamed in terror and his mother came out of the tent and took him in her arms to quiet him.

By this time the rain was coming down so fiercely that we found it almost impossible to walk from tent to tent. We stopped in Josef's " office," another tent, to wait for a calm spell in the storm. I sat on a bench at one side near where water was dripping steadily from above, while Josef worked with a little benzine stove which was out of order. After a while he made it flame up cheerfully, and when that happened he shoved the stove toward my bench so that I could thaw out a little before the flame died away again.

" This tent is better than any of the others," he observed while he worked.

Presently three men came in, one weeping, and all in great distress. Josef talked with them, while they gestured and expostulated in Arabic, wringing their hands. He shrugged his shoulders and spread both hands wide open in front of him. I knew that meant, " No — I am sorry, the answer is no, and I can't do a thing about it." They went off muttering and weeping.

" Their tents were blown down in the wind early this morning," Josef explained to me. "They can't be repaired and we can't supply them with others."

I asked him if the men had families and he said they had — ten in one, six in another, and three in the third.

"But what are they going to do?" I asked.

He shrugged his shoulders again, not indifferently but helplessly. "They can send the children around to other tents," he said. "I have told them to do that. The older ones will manage somehow without shelter. It is a pity."

"Isn't there anything else they could have, if there aren't tents?" I asked.

"Certainly. They could have mud huts. But what would happen to a mud hut on a day like this?"

We looked out into the pouring rain again, and I remembered some of the mud houses I had seen, leaking, crumbling, with water seeping in around the sides, never drying even in the short periods of sunshine.

"The mud huts are all right for Jericho. It never rains there," Josef said. "Jericho is the place for the higher classes. These should go to Jericho for the winter, don't you think — as our wealthy Jerusalem people used to do in the old days." He laughed a little bitterly.

"Well, at least I shall be getting out of all this myself," he said then. "Six months — and then four years of freedom in America."

I asked if he would be coming back then and he shrugged again.

"Who knows? Not if there is any other way. There is nothing here to come back to. Nothing except poverty and cold and hunger."

"Maybe your people need you," I suggested, and he looked at me, not very kindly.

" Do you know who are the only ones that can help my people now? " he demanded. " They are the Americans! We're helpless to help ourselves. Those of us who can leave must do it because we are probably the only ones of the Palestinians who will live to carry on the race. This is a dying world. Dying in body and dying in spirit."

" It didn't sound so when the man held the child to me," I said.

" That is the death cry of a destroyed people," he said to me. " You have a saying (we Arabs are very fond of sayings, by the way) ' Whom the gods destroy they first drive mad.' That is the mad cry of the Palestinian Arab before he dies."

It was hard to believe that all this happened, is happening, a mile or so from the spot where the Prince of Peace was born. When we drove back into the little town of Bethlehem, and saw a group of tourists in front of the Church of the Nativity, it seemed to me they were trying to look at another world, which had nothing to do with the real world of today.

Later, in the home of Josef's fiancée and her family in Bethlehem, there was still another world to see — that of the more fortunate refugee group, struggling valiantly to make the best of a bad situation, and thankful for the chance to work. The girls were stenographers with UNRWA, earning very small wages, and trying to build some kind of a future for themselves on a few piastres a day. They were trying not to remember, except as remembering could give them dignity for the present, a time when they could afford to be young and gay and self-confident.

Josef's fiancée thought it was a good idea for him to go to America.

" Four years are a long time," I said. " Why don't you get married first? "

" Josef must be free," she said simply. " A wife, even across the world, is a burden to him." She thought for a moment. " If Josef waits for me, it is good. If he marries in America — then he marries."

Then she smiled.

" But he will wait for me," she said. " I will manage here somehow. I am sure that Josef will wait for me. If he were an American, or if he were a British, or if he were a Jew, it would be different. But Josef is an Arab! "

CHAPTER EIGHT

Amirah

Gaza is that small strip of land on the southeastern corner of the Mediterranean coast with Israel on the north and east and Egypt on the south. In the old days Palestine included Gaza, but at the close of the active war between the Jews and the Arabs, this small strip was left unconquered by the Jews and is now under Egyptian military control.

Most of the Gaza strip is desert. It has no industries whatsoever, and no developed natural resources; yet since the Jewish-Arab war, 204,000 Arab refugees from the north have been added to an already poor population. These refugees have received some food and shelter from UNRWA, but all administration of these funds is handled by the Egyptians.

The most direct route from Jerusalem to Gaza would have been straight across Israel by U.N. plane. But the Egyptian government requested that I go by way of Cairo, rather than direct from Jerusalem. So that is the way I went, first to Cairo, and then to Gaza by train across the desert and over the Suez Canal.

There was considerable tension at the time between the Egyptians and the British in the Canal Zone, which added some excitement, and provided a night on the desert. Except for the long time it took, it was one of the most interesting train rides of my life, and it made me acquainted with Amirah.

To be one lone American boarding a train in the great Cairo station is a dubious adventure. It is something like struggling through woods where the trees are dark men, each wearing a white gown and tarboush, and all shouting half in Arabic and half in English, insisting that you buy chocolate, chewing gum, newspapers, anything. Yes, it was a kind of bad dream come true. I was worn out by the time the struggle was over, and fell into the train compartment, still trying to avoid the arms and hands that reached through the open window with chocolate and chewing gum and newspapers and postcards.

Suddenly the forest separated, to admit one of the most beautiful girls I've ever seen, carrying a wicker basket and a paper bag full of small bananas and a cardboard box. Behind her came a black, worn suitcase bigger than the porter who carried it. She tossed him two piastres, half the tip I'd paid and for which I had been grumbled at. Yet her man went away apparently satisfied.

She distributed her parcels, sat down and then smiled at me and said in perfect English, " How do you do? You are the American going to Gaza. I am glad to meet you. I am Amirah and I am at your service."

" Thank you! " I said to the genie of the lamp, having long since ceased to be surprised at the way everybody in the east knows everything. " Can you get rid of the salesmen outside? "

She turned to the window, said a curt word or two in Arabic, and miraculously our compartment was deserted and so quiet that I felt a second of lonesomeness.

" They follow the Americans because all Americans are rich," she observed. " I shall protect you. I am a professional woman. I am a nurse and I too go all the way to Gaza."

The train began to move slowly as she spoke. For a few minutes we sat without talking, and looked occasionally at each other but mostly at the moving scene outside where Cairo was soon left far behind. A thin veil of dust sifting through the air of the compartment assured us that we were on the edge of the desert.

" It is a bad journey. A bad train and a bad ride to Gaza," she volunteered at last.

I said that we ought to be there by nine in the evening, according to the timetable, but she shook her head.

" Midnight. Or early morning. Not at nine," she said firmly. It was a dreary prospect, but it was settled.

We did not talk much for a time, even after that bright beginning. I was concerned with the sand in my nose and my mouth when it was open, and in my eyes too, for it came thicker and faster as we rode farther out over the desert. And I was spellbound with a sea of sand gleaming white for miles and never a house or a tent.

After what seemed a long time the train came to a stop, the porter entered the compartment and closed the window shutters because, he said, we were passing the British camps. When he was gone and the train began moving again, Amirah promptly opened the shutters.

" I wish to see," she observed.

I asked her what we would see, and she told me we'd see the British. But the " British " as we saw them were not exciting — only a few scattered barracks and a volley-ball game. The porter returned to open the shutters, saw that they were already opened, and retired without comment.

Presently I was enchanted with the most heavenly sunset that even the desert can exhibit. The horizon looked far and yet near. The sky was not red but a most delicate pink, reflected on the white sand of the desert. And the sun, which in one minute slipped down out of sight, was replaced in the next by a glowing rose bowl over our heads.

" It is very beautiful! " She entered my thoughts. " But in a moment it will be black night."

Almost as she spoke the night was black with never a star

— the only thing, it seemed to me, that happened fast in the Orient.

Then Amirah closed the shutters again, and smiled at me.

" We have seen the British and we have seen the sunset," she said. " Now we shall see us. You go to Gaza to visit the Arab refugees? "

I admitted it.

" Please try to understand the Arabs," she said. " No one tries to understand them, it seems."

Then she told me about herself.

" I am a modern woman," she said seriously. " A most modern woman, although born of a strict family. I am a nurse in Gaza. Most Egyptian women do not have professions. But I am a modern woman and a Christian, and I go to Gaza to serve the refugee people. I love very much the Arab refugees from Palestine. That is why I hope you will see other things besides what you will see."

It was clear from the light in her dark and lovely eyes that she really loved the refugees.

" What do you do exactly? " I asked.

" My position is that of head nurse at Rafah camp," she said proudly. " I act for the doctor, too, because he comes only once a week, and there is always sickness in Rafah, with 7,000 people. I prescribe the medicines."

She was mildly surprised at my astonishment, and went on to say that she diagnosed and prescribed for all the common diseases, scabies, trachoma, worms and dysentery, and even for tuberculosis. Tuberculosis, she said, was an enemy of nearly every family, and every refugee in all the tent camps of Gaza suffered from malnutrition. She also conducted pre-natal and well-baby clinics and others for children over two years of age. In addition she often delivered a hundred babies a month.

" But isn't it too bad for them to have so many babies? "
I asked her. She opened her black eyes wide, indicating
wonder at that.

" They all have babies," she said. " All Arab families
have many babies. I am trying to teach them to let the doctor
come," she went on. " These people have not had doctors or
midwives and it is hard for them to learn that this is right."

" But if they don't have doctors or midwives, then who delivers their babies? " I asked her.

" The mother delivers her own child," she explained.
" The youngest as well as the oldest. It is the custom. The
mother goes into her tent alone when she knows the time has
come, and stays there until the baby is born. Then she calls
to her husband and announces that she has borne him a son
or a daughter. Only then may he go to his wife.

" But I am trying to teach them. At the beginning only
one and two, and then another would come to me and break
the custom, to have her baby born in the hospital room. But
then these told others, ' Go to Amirah. Amirah will care for
you. It is right what she does.' And now many come. It is
slow but there is change.

" And in the beginning they did not wash the babies. That
is not because the Arab people are unclean, but they feared it
would harm the baby to be washed with water before he was
old and strong. I have persuaded them. They see that it is
good, too. They tell others. That is the way to learn."

I said that they must like her very much.

" There are many small Amirahs in Rafah," she said simply. " They pray to Allah that their little ones may grow to
be like Amirah, and I am Christian and it makes me happy! "

I suggested that they must also be grateful, but she shook
her head.

" I do not think they are grateful. The Arabs are an old

and proud people. No man is grateful for what he must learn in such a way. But I do not wish for gratitude. If by being ungrateful they retain their pride I am glad."

"But anyway they learn," I said. "And even if it comes in a backhanded way, and even if they don't like it, still by losing their homes they've been pushed into a place where they've found at least one advantage. The war at least has done that much good, hasn't it?"

She considered that with the thoughtful attention Arabs make so flattering. When she spoke at last it was evident for the first time that English words were coming with difficulty out of thinking that must have been in Arabic.

"War is not good," she said slowly. "Medicine and new health practices are good. But they should be learned through peace and by choice. When they are forced through war they carry with them the bad feeling of war. But even if that were not so, those advantages do not make up for what they lost in war.

"I do not mean only that they must live in tents now. Many of them have always lived in tents and most of them have been poor. Some of them have had their own small farms. You must try to understand the Arab people. I think you have not heard the truth in America. I think you do not know these people."

I admitted that in America we hear very little about the Arabs. "But we know they aren't all Bedouins riding horses and camping on the desert — if that's what you mean," I said.

"That is not what I mean," she answered mildly. "Some of these people had little pieces of land which belonged to them. But there was the big land which also belonged to them and to their fathers and their grandfathers before them, and the tombs of their ancestors are there. For thirteen centuries they have claimed this land as their own and they were a free people.

" If they preferred to dwell in tents and to move from place to place they were free to do that. It was a part of their freedom that they might own no single piece of earth but own the whole at will.

" For others the little piece of soil they tilled with the house they built was their home. And for them also Palestine was the homeland and they were all a free people. If they chose to break the soil they might do so. And some Arabs had orange groves better than any in the world, and good farms. If they chose to let the land lie untended they were free to do that also. There is nothing so good as to be free," she concluded. " I do not know whether I have made myself clear."

" You have," I said. " But I don't altogether agree with you. Surely it isn't right that anyone should be free to waste land, as you say. It follows that if he doesn't use it, he will eventually lose it. That's the way nature works. I don't know whether I make myself clear," I added.

" I do not understand you," she admitted. " But I am sure you are very wise, only sometimes I do not understand English very well. It seems to me you are saying it was right for the Jews to take the land of Palestine from the Arabs because the Jews would make better gardens. Arab people are very simple. They believe that the land belongs to them because it is theirs — that is all.

" And these advantages that the UNRWA brings to the refugees — the Arab claims the right to choose whether he will have even these advantages. Perhaps in his ignorance he may choose what is not good for him. But he has himself chosen. That is important. Perhaps there is a longer way of helping these people to learn. Perhaps a few among them, having learned of their own choice, will tell a few more to choose and at last they will all choose the advantage."

" But that takes forever," I argued. " There isn't time. They'd all be dead. And while we wait for ' the advantage,' as you say, to catch hold by accident, the women are dying in their tents, delivering their own babies. What good is it to them if they're dead? "

She smiled sadly.

" I wonder if the west can ever understand the east. The Americans want to do things now, today, at once. You want to see them happen. But what difference does it make? And what small things you want! What are one or two or a dozen or a hundred or even a thousand single lives if you save them, but also cause the broken spirit of a proud old people? "

" But the whole world is moving fast," I insisted. " We've got to live in the world right now. And this freedom you talk about — you Arabs never have been free, it seems to me. In America we believe in freedom. It's the basis of our democracy. Our Declaration of Independence says that all men are created equal — "

For the first and only time Amirah broke the eastern rule by interrupting me. Her eyes sparkled.

" That I do not understand," she said. " I would be glad for you to explain to me what you mean about all being equal."

" It means that we're all the same. We all have the same opportunities," I said fumbling for words. It had suddenly become a little difficult to explain equality.

" And is everyone just alike? " she asked. " It seems very strange. Do all have the same opportunities? "

" Well, as a matter of fact — no, that is not yet," I admitted. " But we ought to. We think it's right."

She raised her straight black eyebrows high and her forehead wrinkled. I looked for irony but there was none.

"I am confused," she said. "It is all very confusing."

I apologized for explaining so badly, but added that I thought that was what freedom meant.

"I see," she said. "We have different meanings when we speak of freedom." Then she smiled. "You are very smart in America. And of course I do not expect you to be the same as the Arabs. But I hope that you will try to understand the Arabs."

"Perhaps understanding begins with liking," I said humbly. "I like the Arabs very much."

She smiled.

"The Arabs like the Americans very much," she said. "They do not like your government, but they like Americans."

The discussion seemed to have ended, and I was left with the feeling that somehow my answers didn't add up to the right answer. And I felt that Amirah must be wrong, but she seemed to have won the argument. I found myself wondering if Amirah was only being polite when she said the Arabs liked Americans. I had the uncomfortable feeling of having forced a direct issue which one must not do in the Orient.

The train had stopped for a long time and I told myself that the slow train to Arkansas had nothing on the Cairo-Gaza express. But still this was the land of Samson and Delilah and the dust was romantic dust. About 12:30 in the night we crossed the Canal. Amirah opened the shutters so that we could look out as we went over the bridge, which is technically against the rules, but nobody came to object. There was nothing much to be seen in the darkness. An encampment of the British was close to the bridge on one side. As the light from our window struck them, we saw little clusters of Egyptians, not soldiers, at the side of the tracks. It took exactly three minutes to make the crossing after waiting for seven hours to do it.

After that we settled down for the night. Sometime before it had begun to rain — which was all wrong, because it was March and the rainy season should have been over. But it rained anyway and was getting colder, with an icy wind coming up through the floor. The continuously seeping sand and dust by this time had made a white coat over everything in the compartment, including ourselves. I felt and looked like one of those free Bedouins she had talked about, but Amirah continued to be composed and beautiful.

" I suppose it will be morning," I observed impatiently. " Eight hours late! "

" Certainly it will be morning," she replied. " And now for myself I shall use the sack of bananas for a pillow as Jacob used the stone, and I shall put the coat about me — so." She put her coat about her and lay lengthwise of the seat, with her head on the bananas, and looked like Cleopatra.

" It will be morning. But then there is always tomorrow, perhaps with a sunrise. Why should Americans be in a hurry to get places? Here — there — now — tomorrow — it is really all the same! "

CHAPTER NINE

Mustafa

In Jerusalem and Bethlehem it had been possible to shake off some of the official red tape, but Gaza was different. Mr. and Mrs. Azzam, my hosts, were refugees from Haifa; but they were among the most fortunate because not only had Mr. Azzam been able to salvage some of his former wealth from what is now Israel, but he also had a good job with Barclay's Bank. They had built the house they lived in, a modern stucco bungalow at the edge of what was evidently a new residential area. The whole area was in the midst of the desert, a mile or two out from the town of Gaza and looking straight to the sea.

Between the house and the sea there was a tent village. It seemed only a short walk from the Azzam garden. But I was warned early not to make any excursion to the camp without an escort, which was to be provided by the Egyptian army.

Faithfully the army station wagon, with a lieutenant and usually one or two U.N. officials as well, and the driver, would pull up in front of the Azzam garden to take me on an excursion. These went with me to every camp in the Gaza strip — there are eight — and on a number of occasions to the northern border of Gaza, which is No Man's Land. Beyond that is Israel. There were no barriers, no sandbags on this frontier, and no barbed wire as in Jerusalem. The fields on the north were quiet and well kept. There were men plowing on the other side of No Man's Land, the Israeli side.   It looked very peaceful.   We saw no soldiers at any time.

" I could walk across there so very easily," I remarked once to Lieutenant Hassan, when we stopped to look across the frontier.

" You would not be able to walk back," he told me.   " You would be dead."

Evenings in Gaza were social, because here in the midst of the desert it seemed important to have parties, and even a very modest visitor was an excuse for several.   They were exotic, with exciting guests, most of them Egyptian soldiers and members of the international staff whom I met during the day as officials; and there were incredible pastries and there was incense and oriental music.

One afternoon there was an invitation to tea with Captain Mustafa, who in the morning had overwhelmed me with his dignity as an officer and surprised me with his casualness at a canasta party at night.   This time he appeared in his garden, wearing a blue afternoon coat which looked so gorgeous that I was encouraged to break the rule and try to get down to brass tacks with an oriental.

Over the lemonade and pastries I confessed that I wasn't equal to the pomp and ceremony in Gaza.   I said I admired the uniforms, was charmed with the way Egyptian soldiers click their heels and salute, and grateful for the privilege of meeting so many important people, but that I'd already read in the newspapers most of what they'd said and I wanted to meet *people*.

I said that American young people weren't interested in offices and parades of soldiers, and probably would not be deeply touched by miles of tents and thousands of refugees, and hundreds of clinics and hospitals and schools, schools, schools.   I said they'd want to know somebody, some one or two or three people, how they might be thinking and how they might be feeling.

Captain Mustafa looked shocked. Then he looked distressed. Then he was amused and finally he was serious.

" Would they be interested," he said at last, " perhaps in knowing an Egyptian officer — a captain? How he thinks — how he feels? One who is in a certain manner of speaking — a refugee? "

With great enthusiasm I said that *they* might, and *I* certainly would.

" What would you like to know about me? " he asked. " I never say anything that means anything to anybody. Perhaps you do that in America. It is a strange country." He laughed. " Well, what shall I tell you about myself? "

I told him about the questions which I had asked the children of Damascus. " I wonder if you'd answer in the same way," I continued.

" Possibly," he said. " Since we are being western this afternoon, I must tell you that I don't understand Americans. I dislike them. American women I find unattractive and too intellectual. I have not known very many, of course. But one thing I admire about your people is that you are determined to get what you want and you do get it. But then when you get it, it seems you have changed your mind."

" The orientals don't, then? " I asked.

" Not in the same way and not at once. We wait. We connive, we listen, and we don't think in terms of this lifetime. One is a part of history. The answer or the reward will come perhaps in some other lifetime."

" You expect to be here — in some other lifetime? "

" Perhaps — who knows? But we do not hurry. And in the meantime we are philosophers. We consider many things. We consider what is the reason for living, for instance. And

that question gives us something to think about for as long as
we live, because we never answer it.

" On the other hand the western mind works differently.   I
will say to you, ' Let us consider the reason for living,' and
you, an American, will have a reason.   You will say what it
is, and that is the end of the discussion — poof! "

" What is your reason for living? " I asked him.   He gestured impatiently.

" How like an American! " he said disgustedly.   " Everything out in the open, everything straight from the shoulder —
is that what you say?   It is so uninteresting!   But since you
ask me, suppose I consider — it might be because the flowers
bloom in my garden.   It might be because there is always another spring.   It might be — it might very well be because I
do not know what comes after life.   But — "

He hesitated for a long time.

" I can see that you wish to know what I consider my reason
for living.   And I can no more tell you directly than I can
tell the number of the stars or the sands on the desert.   But
I can tell you how I was a captain in Egypt because my father
was an officer, and how I lived with wealth, and was proud of
my prowess as a rider and somewhat celebrated."   He smiled
modestly.   " And how I was an actor in the cinema, and
played in a famous picture.   You have seen it no doubt, *An-
tony and Cleopatra*, made by the side of the Sphinx? "

I had not seen it, and I think he was rather unhappy about
that.   What he said was, " You astound me, not because *An-
tony and Cleopatra* was a good picture; it was poorly made
and bad in every way.   But it was my impression that all
Americans are familiar with all the cinemas in existence.
Well — I must continue with the story of my life since you
wish to hear it.   I was then sent to Gaza.   Now you may know
that no Egyptian comes to Gaza willingly.   It is the end of

the earth. It has nothing that Cairo has — no comfort, no beautiful women, no society, no dancing. It is utterly barren. When I received the orders to come to Gaza I was distressed because I thought, ' Nothing but desert sands and poor refugees! I shall certainly die.'

" But one does not answer a command except by obeying. I came. And I have been here two years. And there is nothing here except desert sands and poor refugees. The sand I have turned into a garden."

He gestured, and I looked at the rows of sweet peas, the roses and carnations, and the green grass and the trees — an oasis in the desert.

" It is beautiful, is it not? And I have seen men live who would have died except for the small service which I was able to do. For the first time in my life — I am not very old, but I am old enough to have learned some things — for the first time I have been glad to be alive."

There was no answer to make to that. We did not speak, but he clapped his hands and a dark boy in a white gown ran out to the table carrying a telephone. Captain Mustafa plugged in the telephone and made a call in Arabic. Then he apologized.

" Excuse me," he said. " The message was necessary on account of your excursion. All is prepared. Lieutenant Hassan will call at 5:30. And so — we were speaking of life. I have told you about my own life. Now let us consider the whole world. You have seen thousands and thousands of poor refugees, and you are not touched because there are too many. Were you afraid? "

I admitted that I would have been afraid except for the escort.

" The refugees are afraid too," he said. " They are afraid they will die. I think the whole world is frightened. If

Lieutenant Hassan did not wear his uniform in the camps those frightened people there would kill him. All the people you see hide behind their ' pomp and ceremony,' as you call it. Can you not see that the men in the uniforms, the officers, the officials — all of them are frightened people? That is why they wear uniforms, to keep them from being afraid. A uniform makes one safe.

" All are frightened. The rich are afraid of the poor. The poor are afraid of the rich. The King of Egypt is afraid of the people. The people are afraid of the King. And what happens after that? Hate. The Egyptians fear the British. The British are afraid of losing Egypt. They are hiding behind their Empire because they are afraid. The whole world is afraid of America. America is afraid of — "

" Communists," I supplied.

" Exactly. And the Communists are afraid of Democracy. Everybody fears America. Everybody hates America. Everybody hates and fears and distrusts everybody else, and so on it goes.

" It is a pity, is it not? You and I, for example, might be friends except that you are an American and I am an Egyptian and therefore we must fear each other."

" But I hold no threat for you! " I exclaimed.

" Not now. Not here in this garden. Therefore while you are here in the garden we can be friends. Tomorrow I hide behind my uniform. And you — you must have a bouquet of flowers and a rose for your hair."

He clapped his hands. The dark boy in a white gown ran out from the house and hurried about gathering a bouquet. Captain Mustafa himself chose a particularly lovely rose and I pinned it in my hair with a bobby pin.

" Only an oriental woman can wear a rose," he observed critically.

" Can't individuals break down the barriers? " I asked him.

" Little by little as more and more learn to trust each other, perhaps it could be nations."

" It is a nice theory and it sounds like an American speaking. What talkers you are! And how your actions belie your speeches — your good kind speeches! But here is a better theory. And it is practical. If there should be a riot in Cairo when you get there and if you can do so before you are killed, you may present this card and it will protect you because I shall already have written a letter to Cairo to say that you are a ' good ' American."

" That sounds very practical," I said. " Not that I expect to need the card."

Gravely he took a card from his pocket, wrote a few words on the back and handed it to me. I rubbed the lacy Arabic lettering on the other side thoughtfully and noted that it was engraved.

" The Arabic for my own name," he explained.

" This is only an example of what I suggested myself," I said. " Perhaps we really mean the same thing. Perhaps we're really just the same ourselves and only divided by an idiom after all."

He smiled.

" An idiom — and many thousands of years of history. It is a pretty remark. It might be put into a couplet — an oriental couplet."

At that moment Lieutenant Hassan drove up in the station wagon and there was a good deal of saluting and heel clicking. In spite of the blue jacket Captain Mustafa was a captain again.

" See that the lady has a chance to talk to the people," he said curtly. " See that she is left free to go where she wishes and stay as long as she likes. She does not like to have so many people around her and she does not wish to be interfered with. Stay near by — but not too near."

CHAPTER TEN

Spring in Gaza

Except for the seas of white sand on both sides and the long horizon of the blue Mediterranean ahead, Remal camp could have been Seymour, Indiana, at county fair time.

The miles of tents looked neat and adequate in the sunshine. The market with vegetables spread outside, and meat carcasses hanging in bloody but prosperous-looking rows, the seeds and the carpets and brasses, made it a miniature Damascus bazaar. And the swarms of dark people trooping up and down, the women carrying huge jugs on the tops of their heads, the men fingering Moslem bead strings — all seemed to have some place to go. There was laughter among the little crowd that flocked along beside us. There was merriment. Lieutenant Hassan talked with them, and they answered and chuckled.

The heavy shadow of despair that had clamped down against my heart for three weeks began to lighten. " In Gaza," I said to myself, " the people are busy. They are gay." And over all, the bright fresh spring sunlight poured kindly.

Some distance away we saw a crowd of men lounging on the side of a small sand hill, not sleeping apathetically or pretending to, but talking with animation about something. We heard an occasional hearty guffaw.

Below them in the sand valley was a group of women making a bright, multicolored spot against the white sand.

We heard strange oriental music, monotonous, weird, fast, a single phrase repeating itself again and again and then ending abruptly, ending but hanging unfinished in the air as another phrase began to be repeated.

We stopped to watch, and Lieutenant Hassan exclaimed in delight.

" We are lucky today! " he said. " It is a wedding party. You shall see the dancing! "

He started on ahead as briskly as he could over the sea of sand, and I waded after him, feeling the sand rush in to fill up my shoes.

" But if it's a wedding," I said breathlessly, " maybe we shouldn't interfere! "

" Why not? " he called back. Not a question, but a statement, another of those distinctly eastern expressions meaning, " Don't be foolish." We plowed on in the shifting sand.

When we had almost reached the party he turned and said abruptly, " Here is where I must leave you. I am not allowed among the women." Before I could answer he was on his way, climbing up the hill to where the group of men lounged and laughed.

I hesitated, looked toward the men and my escort, and then back toward the women. It was clear that if Lieutenant Hassan was not allowed among the women, I should myself be unwelcome among the men. Somewhat doubtfully I plowed down into the valley alone.

By this time I could see that in the midst of the crowd there was a small circle, and in the center of the circle two women were dancing, and another woman on the edge of the circle beat a strange kind of drum with her fists while the whole crowd joined in the singing or chanting that made the weird thin tune we heard.

There was no question about the welcome in this crowd.

Apparently the women thought I was the funniest sight they'd seen for a long time. They roared with laughter, they crowded around me and almost ignored the dancers in the center because they were so much interested in feeling my coat, examining the bracelet I wore, pointing at my shoes and even pulling my hair which they seemed to be trying to make longer like their own. But it was all in the best of fun.

I was just as interested in their clothing, for it was apparent that they were dressed up for the party. As soon as they knew that, they crowded close to show me their costumes. The embroidery was exquisite, of very fine cross-stitch in intricate patterns and brilliant colors. Seeing the many different patterns, I realized that these women represented a number of different Palestinian villages, each with its own embroidery pattern. The variety was wonderful.

As soon as we had all looked each other over and done a good deal of laughing and smiling and bowing, they made room for me to come up to the center of the crowd and stand in the circle while the dancing was resumed.

Although the dancers changed places now and then, there were always two in the center while the group chanted and occasionally yodeled and one woman beat on the drum. The drum, seen up close, looked like a large earthenware jug or jar with a piece of animal skin stretched across the top. We all kept time together, and I stamped my feet on the sand along with the others. One couldn't help it, for the rhythm was contagious. It seemed to take possession of one's body.

One of the two dancers brandished a sword while she shuffled about in a squatting position. The other kept up a continuous rhythmic quivering kind of shimmy dance, always just out of reach of the sword. Occasionally the one with the sword swept it around the edge of the circle so close that I jumped back when it came my way and they all screamed with joy.

It was altogether the gayest occasion I had seen in any of the camps, and it seemed to be the kind of thing that would go on for hours. But for me there had to be an end. Out of the corner of my eye I saw Lieutenant Hassan standing on the edge of the crowd of men on the hill. He looked as though it were time to be moving along. Reluctantly I pushed my way through the circle and the crowd while they tried to hold me back and the children clung to my hands. The lieutenant met me half way up the hill.

" And how did you enjoy the dancing? " he asked me.

" It was wonderful, but I couldn't make out who was the bride, since they all looked like brides."

" There is not one bride," he said. " There are four. But of course you did not see them. They were not there."

It was odd that a bride wouldn't be at her own wedding celebration.

" They wait in their tents for the husbands to come to them," he said. " It is the custom."

The four grooms had been in that group of men sitting on the hill. The grooms missed nothing. I said it hardly seemed fair to shut the brides off from the fun, but Lieutenant Hassan said they didn't object. They really preferred waiting in the tents, he thought.

I said it seemed to me things looked pretty good in Gaza, and that either these people were really enjoying things here or else they'd made a remarkably good adjustment to a bad situation.

" After all, it is spring," he said. " Nothing is so bad in the spring. But the winter has been hard. Two weeks ago the storms destroyed a hundred tents. The water flooded the

valley between the hills of sand where the women were dancing."

" Do you mean that there were tents there in that place two
weeks ago? " I couldn't believe it.

" More than forty," he said.

" And the families — "

" They were scattered here and there among the other
tents which still stand. They are crowded."

The understatement shocked me.

" And sick," he added. " Twenty people died, four of them
but newly born."

We were back in the tent area now and passed at that moment close to a tent where a child was crying. Then we saw
that it was sick and vomiting while the mother quietly held
its small body. I saw that the child was spitting blood. I
looked at Lieutenant Hassan, but he did not stop.

After we had gone by he said, " It is a pity. There is
nothing to be done."

We went on, and our crowd of followers went with us. No
one looked back to where the child still cried.

The sun shone brilliantly over the sand and the tents.
From far away coming to us over the softest breeze, we could
hear the chanting of the women at the wedding celebration.

" And now you shall meet the children," Lieutenant Hassan said. He turned to the little crowd around us and spoke
a few words in Arabic.

" I am asking them to send us boys and girls who speak
English," he told me.

By some sort of quick grapevine the word went far and
wide, and the crowd around us soon grew so large that we
seemed like pied pipers. And we were showered with a
strange variety of conversation in English. Some of it I
could understand.

" We had a house! " I heard it many times. " We lost our home. We cannot forget."

It was all very confusing, but at last I found the boy I wanted to talk to standing quietly back among the others. He seemed interested but not deeply concerned. He was extremely handsome, dark, tall for his eleven years, with sparkling black eyes and a good-humored smile. He looked even a little amused by the excitement of the others, and did not seem to care whether or not he was noticed.

" That one," I said to Lieutenant Hassan. " That handsome one who doesn't make any fuss — does he speak English at all? He is the one."

The others in the crowd backed away as Bashir was drawn out of his place and presented to me. He spoke a few words of English and he was agreeable. He seemed completely unselfconscious and unimpressed with the honor of his selection. There was about him a dignity and graciousness I found in so many Arab people, even in young children.

Following close at his heels was another little boy, who kept saying insistently, " You see *me!* I am Muhammed. I am Bashir's friend. I speak English. I know all about Bashir."

With Bashir and perforce Muhammed, and with Lieutenant Hassan following, but several paces behind (no doubt because Captain Mustafa had commanded him), I walked along to the tent where Bashir's family lived, and learned about them on the way. Once we stopped and sat down on a rock, so that I could write down what they were saying.

His father had been a baker in Magda, a village not many kilometers from the camp where we were. (Remal is close to the Israeli border.) The family had been quite well off — " rich," Bashir said — and had lived in a house with three floors and fifteen rooms, much elaborate furniture which

Bashir described with enthusiasm, and clothes and jewelry. They had liked to entertain their friends with " the cooking of a sheep over a fire." When he talked about the barbecue, Bashir grew so lyric that he could find no more English words, and lapsed into a flood of glowing Arabic.

" But now," he said, remembering the English, " now there is no sheep! "

Muhammed, who had been standing close by taking in all this, now sat down beside us and joined in the conversation.

" Bashir does not know much English," he explained. " I know all about Bashir and I speak English. The Jews would be coming to Magda and they would kill all the children. The president of Magda sent a message to the people. He said, ' Go to Gaza! ' All the people left Magda."

Bashir said a few words in Arabic and again Muhammed translated.

" We were all walking over the desert because it was not well to walk on the road, so many people. We stayed all night. We slept on the sand."

" Were you frightened? " I asked.

He looked a little ashamed.

" I was frightened," he admitted. And then he added generously, " Bashir was *not* frightened! "

I then asked Bashir about his family. His father, he said, was now a baker in the camp, but the bakery was not as big as the one he had had at Magda. Bashir said that he had two sisters and his mother, and that the family lived in the tent which we could see in the distance.

Bashir said that he wanted very much to become a doctor. He greatly admired the doctor who came to Remal camp once a week; and Bashir said that both his father and mother for many years had wished for him to be a doctor.

At Bashir's home I was impressed with the neatness and

cleanliness there. Remembering the half-cake of soap allowed per person for a fortnight, and the long distance the jugs of water had to be carried from the water center, I marveled that this tent and these people could be so clean.

Bashir's mother was preparing bread dough in a pan, to be taken to the bakery. She scrambled up from the ground to bow to us. She spoke in Arabic, for she knew no English. When Lieutenant Hassan told her she had a fine son, she was delighted. When I admired her lovely small daughter who stood in the entrance of the tent and smiled shyly, she was not so proud. But as Lieutenant Hassan said to me, a daughter is not so important as a son.

The " bakery " only a few steps from the tent was, like the clean tent of Bashir, a hopeful thing to see. The father looked like Bashir, good-humored, agreeable to having visitors, but not overly impressed. Here he had started a small private business of his own, one of the little enterprises which must be characteristic of the initiative and keen business sense of many of the Arab people — an initiative which even four years of moral disintegration could not quite destroy.

Soon after the family had arrived at Gaza, while the rest of the refugees milled about still hoping to return to Magda, Bashir's father had gone into business. He dug a hole in the desert sand, built an oven of mud bricks, and let it be known that he would bake bread for the camp women. He spent his last few piastres brought from Magda to buy kerosene to make the first fire to heat the bricks. The women made their loaves out of the flour rations from UNRWA and brought them on trays or in their hands to the baking oven. For the baking, the baker collected one or two loaves from each batch as pay. (These loaves were round flat discs about the size of a large pancake.)

His accumulation of loaves he carried to the town of Gaza

to be sold in the market there. With the money he received for the bread, he bought from the women in the tents the kerosene allotted in the rations by UNRWA — which they did not need since their baking was done in the bakery. In that way the women had a few piastres, the baker had a few piastres, and the business could go on with mutual profit.

Bashir's family seemed to me by far the most interesting and hopeful I had seen, and I wished to stay longer with them, but Lieutenant Hassan had in mind another boy — he thought a more important boy — whom I should know.

" Your Bashir is a good boy, but he is not an intellectual," he told me. " You have seen too much the laborer."

The bakery seemed to me to be an interesting enough business, but he insisted that he would like me to meet a " real scholar " among the Palestinian refugees and one who would be a professor sometime.

When Younes Kataris was brought to me, apparently hauled out of his school classroom for the interview, I think he was thoroughly frightened. Officials never make this sort of thing easy. One could not help being sorry for him as he stood at attention, small but straight, before a crowd of people which included the headmaster of the school, two teachers, a couple of Egyptian soldiers, the camp director and general supervisor, and myself.

He looked like a child, although he was thirteen, older than Bashir. He saluted the lieutenant smartly. When one of the men offered him a chair, he sat down as if he were not sure it was proper to do so.

Lieutenant Hassan explained in Arabic what we wanted and asked him if he would like to talk with me. He swallowed. One could feel him searching for the English as he replied slowly, carefully, in perfect English, " Yes. Certainly. Shall I speak English or Arabic, please? "

We asked for English. Still carefully choosing his words, he told his story, too nakedly and unemotionally for fiction, almost as if he were making a speech. He spoke so slowly that I took down each word as he spoke.

" My home is in Samson. I lived in a house. Not a big house, but big enough. I am the son of a farmer. My father farmed. My mother baked the bread. I went to school. I was a very intelligent boy. I am now a scholar. I wish to become a teacher. I shall teach the refugees of Jebalia or I shall teach the children of Samson if I go to Samson once again. I have five brothers. Three are older. Two are younger. I have one sister. A baby. I had another brother. He — "

Suddenly he stopped, and his eyes filled with tears. He bit his lips determinedly. Lieutenant Hassan looked at him in wonder. The camp director said compassionately, " See how he weeps when he speaks of his brother! "

" Don't say any more, Younes," I told him. " You don't need to tell me any more."

But at last he was in control of his voice again.

" I wish to continue! " he said firmly. " My brother — my brother — " then he stopped again.

I turned to Lieutenant Hassan and begged him to make the boy stop talking, but he answered briefly. " He wishes to tell you about his brother. Let him do so in Arabic. It is better."

Then Younes spoke in a flood of Arabic, crying at the same time.

" He says that his brother joined the Egyptian army and was made a prisoner in the war. He has not been heard from since."

Lieutenant Hassan stopped and Younes, who had listened intently to the interpretation, said in English, " I hope my brother lives! "

The crowd of men, most of them almost as shaken as I, echoed " We hope so certainly."

We took some pictures of Younes, and gave him a bundle of clothing, including a warm coat that had been made for a girl, although he did not know it. I gave him twenty piastres and sent him back to the schoolroom. The headmaster assured me that Younes is one of the few who have a future to look forward to because he is, as he said, a scholar and will win a scholarship to study.

" He will be all right," the headmaster assured me. " Younes will be a happy man. He is lucky."

It was the end of the day. We went on from there to sit for a few minutes at the officers' club which fronts the sea. The sun was just going down over the Mediterranean, spectacular and crimson.

" I think it is going to America," Lieutenant Hassan said. " All good things are there, and what is good here must go there — if it is to live."

CHAPTER ELEVEN

Israel:
Modern Drama in an Ancient Setting

Although there is no active warfare in Palestine at the present time, the hostility between Arabs and Jews makes it extremely difficult for a writer to visit Israel and the Arab countries on the same trip. I was therefore faced with making a hard choice, in planning the research for this book.

Since I had spent a fortnight in Israel on another fairly recent journey to the Middle East, and since a great deal more is written and known in the Western world about the Jewish refugees than about the Arabs, I finally refused — although with real regret — the gracious invitation of Youth Aliyah and Hadassah to revisit Israel on this occasion.

Next came the question of whether or not the Israeli story must be left entirely out of this book — which omission would of course make for a one-sided presentation of refugee problems in Palestine. The only alternative seemed to be to present some stories from available reports and case records; and this I have done.

The stories chosen and retold here were furnished by Children to Palestine. They are true, and they are about real people, the only difference being that I did not meet and know these people myself, and I did not visit Ben Shemen Village, which is described in one of the records.

I should not like to present these stories, however, without adding at least a warm reference to my own experience in Israel, when I went as a visitor without any plan for writing about places or people. There are certain strong impressions which all travelers in the country seem to carry back with them, and which cannot be forgotten or ignored.

You cannot stay in Israel for two weeks, or one week, or a day without catching deep in your spirit a new belief in adventure, challenge, power, possibility. Regardless of how you may feel about the political issues back of what's happening, you must be thrilled over the dogged determination of these people to *do a thing that can't be done*.

Before your eyes speeds history telescoped, a completely plotted drama of human progress. Here are hundreds of destitute people arriving in a single day from a score of countries of the world, to be regimented, housed, taught a language, trained in a trade or a profession, channeled into city or country settlement, or village or *kibbutz*, on a vast assembly line turning a ragged hodge-podge of divers humanity almost overnight into an organized citizenry. Today a barren hillside, tomorrow a city rising on the same spot; today a rocky desert, next spring waving fields of grain. It can't happen — but it does.

It seems like a vast, improbable dream, or a gamble on which a whole people have staked everything they are with most of the odds against them. The first shots fired in an east-west war might end the dream — or an international decision somewhere, slanted just a trifle in the wrong direction — or a short pause in the generous pouring in of funds from America. A moment's rest from labor — or a slight internal disturbance amongst the varied population of Israel — and the gamble might be lost. It's a race against time to make every flying moment count in every swiftly passing day, without a chance to gauge distances, or measure risks, or look back.

You hear surprisingly little about the war, and you don't hear much about the past. There is much talk of the future — but the future is right in the present. And you hear little of other places or people in the world. In Israel, it seems, there are only *we* and *now*.

You are acutely aware of the fact that you're in a country which badly needs every penny it can get, and more. You read signs about an " austerity program " which refer to the pathetically low subsistence rations allowed Israelis. Prices are sky-high. There is no bargaining. There is no begging. It all fits into the picture of dogged purpose in every moment and every movement of the country.

And over and through it all the big job goes constantly forward. All night long you hear the noise of building. All day long you are swept dizzily from one picture to another, of all kinds of people, doing all kinds of things, in all kinds of places — factories, farms, welfare centers, children's homes, schools, colleges — but always working. Nothing and nobody ever *stops*. You're weary of looking and listening. You feel like somebody old and ineffective in a new world where everybody belonging is young. There are plenty of octogenarians in Israel, but there are no old people. It is the youngest, busiest, noisiest place in the world.

And then abruptly — in the midst of this oppressive, everlasting activity — you are aware, one morning, on waking in your twentieth-century motor-court cabin opened the previous week, of a little girl planting flowers in the bare plot of new earth under your window. You hear singing and laughter. You feel the fresh wind and smell its fragrance across a greensward that lately was rock and sand.

The white-coated boy from Czechoslovakia, who swings along the path with your breakfast tray perched on his shoulder, does not stop in the swift performance of his duties. But while he lays out your herring and marmalade and toast on the table, he tells you briefly (because time marches on) about himself.

" I had lost everything. But it is all here — in my country! "

CHAPTER TWELVE

Ben Shemen Boy

*This true story is from the film " Tomorrow's a Wonderful Day,"
which may be obtained from Children to Palestine.*

I would like to tell you about my village, Ben Shemen.
It's not really a village, but a country school for boys and
girls, near Tel Aviv. It's a place where Jewish children from
all over the world, who have lost their homes, may come and
find a new home, and a place to go to school.

Not everybody here came from a concentration camp as I
did. Maybe that's why Ben Shemen means more to me even
than to lots of the other kids. I never really had a home before. I was born in a Jewish ghetto in Poland, and a ghetto's
not a home, you know — only a sort of storage place, jammed
with people who aren't allowed to live anywhere else. There
used to be many of those ghettos in Europe, I think. I had
a father and mother and a little sister there. When the German army came to Poland we were all sent away to a concentration camp. I was seven years old then.

You've heard about the concentration camps, the barbed
wire, the many families crowded all together into small sheds
or left outside to freeze in the winter. Some of us starved,
and were sick, some were tortured, and some of us were killed,
too. I don't like to remember, but sometimes I can't help it.
It comes back in dreams even now.

But I don't need to tell you about the concentration camps.
My little sister was taken away, but I don't know where they
took her or what they did with her. I hate to think. My fa-

ther was killed by one of the guards. That was when my
mother told me I must escape, because I was young and
smart, and might find my way somewhere to a place where
I'd be free. I was just about twelve, then, I think. Well, I
did escape. I don't know what happened to my mother after
I left. But I escaped, and I got along. I got down into southern Europe, and I got along some way for a long time.

It was about three years after that when I found out about
Israel. I'd never even heard of this Israel before. I thought
Israel was just an old place in the Bible, a long time ago.
But they told me it was a place that belonged to the Jews now,
where you didn't have to sneak around and be afraid, if you
happened to be a Jew. And they told me how Palestine belonged to my people from way back — how the Jews scattered
out over the world, and how they're coming back now to take
possession of their homeland. From all over the world, they
said, we were coming — just the way it says in the Bible.
They told me all that.

Well, I didn't know whether it was true or not. I wasn't
even very anxious to get on that ship that was sailing for Palestine. Because I couldn't imagine anything good in the
world — for me. There never *had* been anything good. But
then I had nothing to lose, and I thought if I was smart enough
to escape from Poland, and to shift around for three years
by myself, I'd be as smart as anybody in Israel. So I let
them bring me here — to Ben Shemen village.

I didn't know how the people at Ben Shemen would feel
about me either, and I didn't care. But I know now, and it
makes me feel good to think of it.

I learned afterward what a lot they had to do to get ready
for us the morning we were supposed to arrive — all the kids
from the ship who were coming from the camps and the ghettos, to the children's village.

There was the food to get in, the chores to finish, and the birds to feed — the pigeons and the chickens. The kids here tell me now that I looked strange to them the day I got off that truck that brought us all from the ship. " You looked like a bird," they said. " But not like one of ours. You looked like a bird with a broken wing."

Well, they washed and made themselves clean and dressed up to greet us, as though it were the Sabbath. They shined their shoes, and made themselves look neat. They sounded the gong for an early breakfast, and some of them even watched the clock, just to be ready to welcome us. I didn't know it all then, but I know it now, because I've watched the clock, and waited to welcome newcomers myself.

But I didn't know a thing about all that when our truck pulled up at the big gate of the village. All I saw was a crowd of people, and I was afraid of crowds. Now I know why they pushed and shoved and ran to help us out of the truck. I tried to tell the others not to trust these people. I was sullen, and confused.

When I stepped down off the truck, somebody tried to take my things. I had everything I owned tied up in a burlap sack and they tried to take it.

" No! " I said. " No! "

The rest of the boys and girls who came in the truck with me walked across the grounds like dumb, blind sheep. It's a habit you can get when you live in a concentration camp. They just sat where they were told. They were used to it. But not me. I knew how to take care of myself. They weren't going to put anything over on me here in Israel.

" Are the fences made of barbed wire here too? " I wondered. " Will it be hard to escape if I want to? "

Because, you see, to me this was just another concentration camp.

Now I know that from the very beginning they realized at Ben Shemen that I would have to be treated in a special way, not like the others. A woman looked at my bag, and at me, and she didn't try to take it the way that boy had. She just turned and led me over to a closet and showed me where I could hide it. I was glad about that because that bag was all I had. It was my own, and more precious to me than my skin. You have to own something — some little thing!

Well, I'm a little ashamed to tell you what happened that first day. You see I stole something — right off, the first day. I started my life at Ben Shemen by stealing. But I think you'd understand if you could have smelled the bread. Bread gets a powerful smell when you've been hungry for years. When I smelled that bread, and when I could get off by myself I went and found the table where they had it on a plate. The first thing I always had done when I could was to store away some bread to keep. That's what I did that first day. I stole three loaves of bread. And I don't think they saw me, but maybe they did. I hid it in my sack in the closet.

You can stand anything, if you have enough bread. Bread keeps, even if it gets hard as a stone. I felt better after that. I had bread.

Well, I went looking around that village. There were a lot of people, boys and girls, and some older people too, but they didn't bother me. They just left me alone to get used to things. It was queer to be able to go wherever I wanted to. I didn't exactly like it. You get used to being told where to go.

That was when I smelled the water, because water smells good. And I found it, a little brook. I thought maybe there might be a road on the other side. I was learning things like that so I could get away quick when I got ready. But all I saw were some ducks and some kids sitting on the bank with their feet in the water. They didn't notice me. But I noticed something. They hadn't any shoes on.

" So they take away the shoes here, too," I thought.

Well, the next thing I found was the place where those birds stayed. I found the henyard. You know, whenever I go into the henyard now I can live over that time. I remember again how Miriam came out of the henhouse that day with a handful of little cheepy chickens. It was as though the sun had made her clear, and not hazy like all the rest of the people.

She didn't see me at first, but I saw her. All the little kids crowded around and made a fuss over those baby chickens. But I looked at that girl Miriam.

" She's awfully pretty! " I thought. " But what does she want? "

Then she saw me and she smiled.

" Why does she smile at me? " I asked myself. " She wants something. Don't trust her. Just keep on looking for an exit."

Then I thought maybe I'd better show up at the school. They told me I was supposed to go to school. I found it pretty soon. I looked in and saw all the kids — all those dumb sheep that came in the truck with me. The teacher was asking them questions. I knew then that something must be up. But I thought I'd better go on in.

" I'll go in," I said to myself. " And I'll sit down if I have to, but you better not say anything to me. Because I won't answer any questions." I've learned. Never admit to being a Jew — even to a Jew. Never say anything except " No! "

I wondered what those kids were saying. Gosh, I thought — that Jugoslav girl! They always talk too much. I couldn't understand what she was saying, but it was too much whatever it was. The next one was André.

" Frenchy," I said to myself, " don't you tell the name of the peasant who hid you! " But André shut up right away. " That's good," I said to myself. " But there go those twins from Italy. They'll ruin it. Listen to them — I bet now comes the whole story — the underground, the partisan school. Clowns! Oh, what's the use? "

Then I thought, " Well, go on! They might as well have the whole story from Holland too." That was when they started questioning Jan. And then they said my name.

I wondered why everybody was looking at me. I wasn't going to tell anything. No matter what they asked I wasn't going to tell. I'd say, " No! " That's all I ever had said, just " No! " and that was all I ever would say — " No."

Well, I kept on saying " No." But everything else in that village seemed to be saying " Yes."

And every time when things got especially bad, I thought it was time to get moving — to find the gate — to get out.

One time after I got to knowing my way around I started down toward the road to leave. I don't know exactly what I had in mind. I don't know just where I was going. But I was confused. And I was scared. I didn't know what I was scared of. Maybe it was just myself, being always just with myself.

I saw some girls dancing and somebody was playing music for them. I couldn't stand that music. My kid sister used to dance like that before they took her away. Even in the camp she would dance, poor kid. She would be about twelve now, judging from the last time I saw her. And I was fifteen now — gosh!

I thought I'd better be getting out of this place. It

shouldn't be hard to get out. Everybody seemed to be so taken up with that crazy dancing. I wished the music weren't so loud. I wished they'd stop it. Those girls hadn't any shoes on either. I wondered why. I wondered how it felt to dance without shoes.

And then, because I couldn't bear all that music and dancing, I thought of my bread. Three whole loaves. What would they do if they found it? They mustn't find that bread! It meant something to me — bread.

The funny thing — but I didn't know it until a long time afterward — was that they did find it! It fell out of the sack on the floor and they found it and they knew. But do you know what they did? They put it back in my sack! I never knew until a long time afterward, and by that time it didn't matter. I understood about Ben Shemen village by that time.

I began to feel lonely, in a way I hadn't felt lonely all of my life. Maybe because everybody was doing something. Even the smallest had something to do. I noticed the new ones who had come with me on that truck were working too. Why did they do it? Why didn't they hate it? Didn't they work enough in the camps?

In the camps we chopped wood too — for coffins. We made iron — for chains. How could they forget so quickly? How could they bear the sound of that hammer? It was worse than the music. I had to get out of that place.

Well, I went out to the field where the horses were. I didn't mind the horses. And that's where small Benjamin found me. He was just a little kid. He told me his name was the same as mine. He was a nice kid. He touched me. I touched him. I wasn't afraid of small Benjamin.

Well, I have no clear memory of how many days it was before the thing happened. They were all so easy with me, but it didn't help. I listened to what they said about this being my home, about this country being my homeland, the way the Bible said, and all that, but it was a lot of words. I began to feel like everything in this village was tied up with something bigger, but it never reached me then.

From behind dark places I often saw the kids running in the sunlight. I heard them sing, and sometimes I found myself wanting to run after them. I even began to envy the nursery children and to wish I could be small again and sit there with a book for the first time, and begin from a beginning.

You see I had forgotten how to read and write. No matter where I began, it always ended in the same place — barbed wire. Sometimes that girl Miriam would be watching me, but that only made it harder. Barbed wire. That's where I always ended.

I could hardly bear it the day Miriam said, " Forget the past. Be like us. Come, let's listen to the music."

Well, I said " No " to her, too, but I wanted to say " Yes." I wanted to, but I couldn't.

It's hard to explain what happened the day they began reaping the wheat. I saw them start off with their scythes, and I thought, " Forced labor again! " They were singing, the fools! I only wanted to get away.

But Joseph confused me. He was talking to the others and then he was yelling to me, " Come and help! Come on! "

He gave me a hoe and walked with me out to the field. I went without really knowing why, I was so confused.

The cattle scared me, and the sight of those bended backs was like touching a raw nerve. The fresh earth reminded me of only one thing — graves.

I know just where it happened, but for the life of me I can't remember the donkey cart — or Jacob — although he must have been there at that time of day — or the cove — nothing!

When the others went to lunch it seemed strange that they should go without a word. Why were they leaving me alone? Was it another trick?

They went over to the corner of the field to eat, of course, and expected me to follow, I guess. But I didn't trust them.

And then — I turned, and walked right by it — by the wire! Right behind the barbed wire! First I didn't see it. Then I did. And suddenly something hit me.

I swear to you I saw the camp. I saw the wire. I touched it. I felt — like somebody in a nightmare. The barn behind the wire became the death house. And my turn was next.

Down it came — the whip — the whip!

And then like a miracle *it* happened. I wasn't going to take it! I was going to fight back!

" No " again — but a different " No."

" This time," I yelled, " this time I'll kill you! I'm strong. I'm smart. I can escape! "

I fought blindly, hitting at that fence with a stick. The cows came through the break in the fence. Dazed, knowing the damage they might do, I hit at them too.

And then I smelled the bread! You can smell bread baking a mile away! Or maybe I imagined it. But that was what brought me out of the fog. And I saw what I had done.

For the first time I saw myself, as all of them were seeing me. For the first time, I understood.

And I, who was fifteen — I, for the first time in seven years bowed my head in the field — and wept!

That night I must have walked for hours, and do you know what brought me back? It was a song — a song we used to sing when we were children. These children were singing it in the parlor that night, together. And I had to come back to the song.

And then it struck me. The prison camp was dead! I killed it myself, that morning. But the song — the song was alive. And the children were alive. And I was one of them!

Well, that's about all of my story. I didn't change all at once, because you can't do that. But I learned to work, with the others. I learned to like them. I learned even to sing with them.

And I learned about this village, and this country. They told me again how Palestine belonged to us, and how the Jews were coming back to claim their homeland. They said it wouldn't be easy, but if we worked hard, and stuck together, we'd change the desert into a garden — our garden — our village — our Israel! They told me all that, and at last I understood. I believed.

That's all. This village will always be my home, no matter where I go, I guess. And this country will be my country, because it has always belonged to me and mine.

CHAPTER THIRTEEN

Vicente From Venezuela

This chapter is rewritten from a story entitled " Vicente " by Hadassah Babttaim, in Clay in the Hands of the Potter, *a collection of true stories from Israel by Eva Michaelis, published by the Department for Child and Youth Aliyah, Jerusalem.*

" Zionism! " shouted old man Minsky. " What's the matter with you, my son? Are you crazy, Vicente? We haven't got good enough malaria for you in Venezuela. So you have to go to Palestine to get it! "

Abraham Minsky had wandered into Caracas, the capital of Venezuela, in 1918. He hadn't much then except a pedlar's pack and a new bride from New York. Abraham had been three years away from the " old country " and had wandered over the United States, peddling, before he came at last to South America. In Caracas they found Hannah was going to have a baby, so they decided to settle down and stay for a while anyway.

That was a boom year in Venezuela because of the opening of the oil field. In only a few months, by working hard Abraham had exchanged his pedlar's pack for a small shop. When their son was born they called him Samuel, and Samuel grew up wanting to be a storekeeper like his father. When he was eighteen he took over the whole business, which wasn't a small shop as it had been, but a large department store.

Vicente was born four years after Samuel. For some reason he was so different that sometimes Hannah wondered if he could possibly be her own son. Maybe that was why he was her favorite boy, too. Perhaps it was his name that made him different, for Vicente was named after the president of Venezuela.

Anyway, for some reason Vicente became completely one with his South American friends. He wasn't interested in being a Jew, and even refused to have any part in the Jewish festivals his family celebrated so faithfully. Abraham and Hannah were worried about that.

" He'll end up by marrying a *shickse*,* you'll see! " Abraham said to her.

In high school Vicente joined the radical Federation of Students. That was the last straw. Even Samuel was worried.

That was really the reason that Samuel and Vicente went one evening to hear a lecture on Modern Palestine.

None of the family were Zionists. Samuel especially was too busy to be concerned with that kind of business. As far as they were concerned Palestine was a place for other Jews to go to, if they hadn't any other place to live. The Minsky family had many times mourned over the fate of the Jews in Europe. They had made large contributions for Jews in Palestine. Yet the idea of a National Home struck them all as fantastic.

Samuel felt this way about it. On the other hand, for Vicente to be ready to forget all the old Jewish customs and become as a Gentile seemed equally fantastic. So Samuel conceived the idea of taking Vicente to hear the lecture on Palestine. He thought it might help his brother to forget some of his radical ideas, and so, although Vicente wasn't at all interested, the two of them went to the lecture.

---

* *Shickse* is a derogatory slang expression meaning " Gentile girl."

They came home from that lecture with some new ideas. Although Samuel had gone only to take Vicente, he was sufficiently impressed to make inquiries and send for pamphlets and leaflets. These caused a good deal of discussion in the family.

Abraham was not at all pleased and said so emphatically.

" It is a mad dream! " he said. " It's only for fanatics. Palestine is a hard place to live in. I have it on good authority that people are starving and dying there by the thousands."

" But it's the homeland of the Jews! " protested Samuel.

" It would never work," Abraham insisted. " How can a Jew make a living from another Jew? "

He patted Samuel's shoulder. " Be content! It's good here. There is a little anti-Semitism here, it's true, but not as much as in other places. If you're careful you can avoid it. Venezuela is a good place to make money."

Then came the election of 1937 with its violent swing to the right. The new government promptly took measures against every radical and liberal they could lay hands on. They arrested the leaders of the radical Students' Federation. Among them was Vicente, then fifteen years old. He was taken to jail with all the others.

Abraham was terrified. He and Samuel went to the police station to plead for Vicente's release. Samuel tried to speak first, but they took no notice of him at all. Then Abraham, in his strongly accented Spanish, burst out.

" He is only a child! " Abraham shouted. " Since when do you send children to prison?"

" Listen, Jew! " the policeman snarled. " You Jews have made plenty out of us. Now we'll get a little back. Give me what you've got on you and bring me some more tomorrow and I'll see what can be done. You better teach your kids not to meddle in what's not their business. It's going to be an expensive lesson! "

In despair Abraham and Samuel went home to Hannah, who was in a state of collapse. Every day they went back with more money and more food. And every day Hannah shut herself up in her room. She would not speak or eat. She only wept and prayed.

A whole week went by before all those who had been arrested — the children and the old people — were released from the prison, and poor Vicente stumbled home. Hannah nearly died of joy then! She could hardly let go of him. How she wept when he told her that for all that week he had had only beans and coffee in his stomach!

" The wardens told me every day about all that food you sent me, which they ate themselves! " he said.

That night the Minsky family all sat around the table and had a long, long talk.

" You know, father," Vicente said, " they took me because I am a Jew. It wasn't because I was a member of the Students' Federation at all. I wasn't a leader, and I never had very much to do with it. Besides, none of the other boys my age were taken. Somebody had a grudge against the Jews and they took it out on me."

Abraham was shocked. " I can't believe it! " he exclaimed.

" They made that pretty clear in jail," Vicente said grimly. " They talked a lot about bloodsuckers and rich heathens who made their money by exploiting the poor innocent Christians."

Vicente's face grew dark. He clenched his fist.

" I was never much of a Jew, father," he went on. " But if it's going to be thrown up into my face like that, I'm going to be more Jewish than Moses. Seriously, father, why should we stay here where we're not wanted? Let's sell up and go where we'll be taken for ourselves, and where it isn't a crime to be a Jew."

Abraham was impressed but he wasn't convinced even then.

" Why don't you go to New York if you don't like it here? " he suggested. " We've got relatives there, and you could get in business with my uncle — "

But before he'd finished speaking they were all startled by Hannah's joining in the discussion. She was usually quiet while the men talked. But this time she joined in.

" When you were born," she said to her eldest son, " we called you Samuel, and I hoped that you would be a rabbi as my father was. But I saw that it was not to be. And this Vicente — " she touched Vicente's hand lovingly — " there was no hope of *his* being a rabbi! But I am determined that if my sons will not serve God directly, they should at least serve their people in the Promised Land."

She paused, and Abraham was about to speak. The boys were too startled to say a word.

" Don't argue with me," she said before Abraham could get the words out. " My mind is made up. If only for my sake they must go. Another week like the last one would kill me."

She sighed, and then went on addressing her husband.

" You and I, father, are too old to uproot ourselves," she said. " But I shall not know a moment's peace until both of our boys are writing to me from our own country."

She was not to be argued with, and indeed set about arranging for Vicente's departure with such vigor that in three weeks he found himself on his way to Panama to register for immigration to Israel with Youth Aliyah.

Not long after that Vincente was writing to his mother from Palestine. In that place he was neither keeping a store nor going to radical meetings. For Vicente became a fisherman. A few months later Samuel went there too, and Samuel's business was selling the fish which Vicente caught. Later on they hoped their parents would come and live with them.

" You see, it only needed one of us to make a start! " said Vicente.

FROM ITALY

CHAPTER FOURTEEN

Born to Sing

Before going to Naples, I had a sidelight on the Italians. It happened at a circus I had seen in Greece with Mrs. Haniatou.

It wasn't much of a circus — just a one-ringer under a ragged tent, with tired-looking elephants, a few disgusted clowns, and some shabby trapeze artists. But a dozen of us rode a rickety bus all the way from Elleniko to Athens to see it.

Furthermore it was an Italian circus. With all the array of languages represented among the dozen of us, there wasn't anyone except Mrs. Haniatou who could say more than " Si, si."

Straightaway there was a mix-up over seat tickets. Mrs. Haniatou advised us to sit tight. Sitting tightly herself in her choice aisle chair, she undertook to argue with the Italian usher, who summoned the ticket seller, who summoned the manager. Mrs. Haniatou tried in turn her Greek, her Turkish, her English, her French, and finally her two or three or a dozen Italian words, none of which seemed to fit. The usher and the manager and the ticket seller tried to reply first in double-quick Italian, and then German, and then their two French words " Attendez " and " Voilà " — which also didn't apply exactly. The rest of us, sitting tightly, listened to a barrage of strange and violent explosives that fell like a hailstorm over our heads.

The argument, for all its fierceness, was never really settled. It ended though when the bell rang, the band struck up a tune and six ugly midgets ran out bearing French placards that read " Voilà " and " Attendez! " The manager threw up his hands and dashed away screaming in Italian, the ticket seller threw up his hands and dashed away screaming, the usher shrugged his shoulders and continued to stand threateningly near us in the aisle, but with only a few futile Italian mutterings.

Mrs. Haniatou threw back her head and roared a great Greek laugh.

" These Italians! " she exclaimed in English. " These lovely, beautiful Italians! " And the tears ran merrily down her cheeks.

" You see," she went on, lowering her voice because the circus was beginning, " we love them very much. To be sure we had a war, but it was never the Italians we hated — never. We loved them all of the time! "

While the elephants and clowns and trapeze artists performed before us, Mrs. Haniatou told me about the Italians.

" The truth is," she said, " it was a mistake for them to fight. From the beginning it was an error. The Italian cannot fight. He knows only how to play."

" But they won, didn't they? " I asked her.

" Won? The Italians won, you say? " She was horrified. " You are wrong, excuse me. The German machines overrode our country. They did not conquer us. But the Italians? It was pitiful! I know. I was there to see it happen.

" They are not like the Greeks," she went on. " We are warriors, and have been since before Achilles. I do not say that it is a good thing. But I say it is a true thing that the Greek soldier is the best soldier in the world. The Italian soldier on the contrary is the worst soldier in the world."

She drew a breath and had to shout now above the noise of the band.

" Always when the battle began and the Greeks rushed out boom-boom with the guns, those Italian boys, those beautiful curly-haired boys, were sitting in a trench some place, playing music, singing a pretty song, and they were never ready with the guns to shoot!

" But how could they sing! And how smart they could be with their singing! There were the women (the Italian women are not so smart, but they too can sing), and they followed their beautiful boys across the border into the very villages of Greece. We let them come because even in a war we Greeks are human still. They stood outside the walls where their Italian boys were our prisoners, and talked to them through the windows until the Greek guards drove the women away. After that the women would stand far off and call to the windows to ask if Angelo were there, or Giuseppe or Pietro. And the Greek guards told them they must not call the men.

" ' Is it permitted then that we sing? ' the women asked. And the Greek guard said it was permitted for them to sing. For who will deny the privilege of song? Not any Greek!

" And what a heaven of song! "

Mrs. Haniatou trilled a tune from *La Traviata*, which just reached me above the noise of the circus band.

" But *what* did those women sing to that tune? It was ' *Ah, my Angelo, are you there?* ' or ' *Pietro,*' or ' *Giuseppe* ' or ' *Giovanni — does the cruel wall enclose my beloved?* ' "

Mrs. Haniatou chuckled reminiscently.

" And they, the beautiful boys sang back — the Verdi music. But what were the words they sang? It was ' *Ah, Maria, your Giovanni is here! With food in his belly, carissima!* ' "

The band was playing a jazzified " O Sole Mio " and I leaned forward to hear the rest of what she said.

" You may see by their fingers if a people are soldiers." She held out her own short square hand to show me. " The hands of the Greeks — see they are square, the fingers thick and short for holding fast the gun. But the hand of the Italian — "

Without looking at him she reached up toward our dejected-looking usher, who was still standing by her chair watching the trapezers. Before he could be surprised, Mrs. Haniatou had yanked off his soiled white glove and thrust the usher's hand under my nose.

" The hand of the Italian — you see the fingers are long. And with points! Such fingers are only for plucking the strings! "

She released him then, and handed back the glove which he put on again with the merest shrug of one shoulder, indicating that this kind of thing happened every day. Then they smiled ecstatically at each other.

" You really like your enemies, don't you? " I observed.

She gasped.

" But *never* were we enemies! " she insisted again. " And what hard heart would not love a people who sing? Fighting between us was never a thing that should be — only a thing that was. But the Greeks and the Italians, soldiers and singers, in their souls they are brothers! "

CHAPTER FIFTEEN

A Palace in Naples

Naples is a big, noisy, dirty city, and the seemingly endless ride from the train station to Portici took me along streets that were narrower and dirtier and more damaged with every tick of the taxi meter. The last mile or so we pushed along through crowded markets, with vegetables and sausages and cheeses brushing the sides of the car, and children swarming around it. There must be no place in the whole world with so many children, and so much noise.

Apparently not many people ever take taxis out to Portici, because my taxi driver didn't know exactly where our destination was, and we both studied the numbers painted on the walls of the buildings to try to find the right one. I found it first, but the driver either couldn't or wouldn't understand when I shouted in English, " Stop! " By the time I'd thought of the Italian word we'd gone on another mile. By the time we had made the long slow trek back, the taxi fare had doubled, and both the driver and I were exchanging unmistakably bad words in two languages. Altogether I was disgusted with all Italy and especially Naples, and more especially Portici, before we finally stopped at Casa Materna.

But Casa Materna — in the midst of rubble and children and little shops and noisy markets — is a palace, a real palace with a doorman and a marble staircase. The change from outside to inside took my breath away as did also the two flights of marble stairs, grandly illuminated with stained glass windows over the landings. It was magnificent!

On the second-floor landing I was met at the large elegant door by Signora Santi, who must be about eighty years old and walks with a cane, but who has an eternally youthful smile. She told me in careful English, " Our home is your home! " I was at once rushed through the large plush-filled living room into a mahogany-filled dining room, and set down in front of a steaming bowl, not of peacocks' tongues, but of hot soup. All this happened in less than two minutes. Although I was tired and still somewhat furious with the taxi driver and not sure where I was, the soup warmed my heart and my feelings. A little later, I thought, I will try to learn what this is all about.

Just then the big door into the dining room swung open slowly, and an old man walked into the room. He looked like Santa Claus, with the warmest, brightest face I have ever seen.

" God bless you! " said Pastor Santi, and with that the last irritation at the taxi driver melted away. I never heard Pastor Santi say any other words in English except those three. He was likely to skip back and forth between Italian and French, sometimes changing in the middle of a sentence. But " God bless you " seemed to be his English vocabulary and it was sufficient.

A little dark-eyed girl whom they called Fernanda brought us plates of spaghetti then, and later bowls of hot milk, and I learned how these Italians drink coffee. They sprinkle a little Nescafé over the top of the milk and drink it from the bowl. I liked it. I liked everything including the Signora's friendliness, the Pastor's blessing, the calm beauty of that lofty dining room, and the faint sound of children's voices that just reached us now and again through a casement window overlooking the garden.

" This place is like a palace," I said. " I've been thinking that ever since I came up those marble steps."

" It *is* a palace," the Signora answered with a pleased smile. " One time lords and ladies lived here. Tomorrow you will see the small princes and princesses who live here now — at school, at play, at meals."

Signora was something like a queen or a duchess herself. The Pastor I thought was more like a saint.

That night I slept on the top floor of the palace, the only resident of the vast expanse of marble corridor and rows of spacious bedchambers. The ceiling in my own room was so high that, after all the lights were off except the small bed lamp, I could scarcely see the top. When I opened the long casement window and walked out onto the balcony, I looked down upon a garden, black and white in the moonlight and fragrant with the first perfume of spring. It was a storybook garden, with box hedges and fountains and palm trees straight out of a fairy tale.

Next morning I walked in that garden, green and blooming by daylight, between rows of palm trees, and watched the children playing among the marble statues. On one side of me the buzz saw screamed from the workshop where the boys were making furniture. In the schoolhouse on the other side there were voices raised in song — Italian song with words I could not understand, but they were joyous.

Fabio Santi, Pastor and Signora's son, the lawyer who handles the business of Casa Materna, came to take me around, and as we walked from building to building, the children called out greetings to him.

" They don't treat you as if you were an official," I re-marked.

" We are brothers," he said. " We are all in the same

family. And we all have our special jobs to do. I handle the business. This boy — " he nodded toward a small, intent youngster hurrying toward the school house — " This boy cuts the bread in the dining room. He is proud to be the best bread cutter in Casa Materna."

A little girl with black eyes and a timid smile came up and put her hand in Mr. Fabio's and spoke to him in Italian. He laughed and patted her shoulder. Then she ran away.

" Carmela says she is glad to be here! " he translated to me. " She came last week from the caves. Her father was killed in the war and her mother is dead now from tuberculosis."

" Does this child have — " I began but Mr. Fabio interrupted.

" No, certainly not. She will be all right," he said. " My brother Teofilo is caring for Carmela's health."

Dr. Teofilo, another Santi, is a practicing physician in Portici and treats the illnesses of all the children in Casa Materna.

" The other sicknesses, those of the heart, are the responsibility of my father and mother, who are also their father and mother," Mr. Fabio said to me. " The effects of war and sickness and homelessness and hunger on young hearts are the worst sicknesses of all. You who have not been through all this cannot know how such losses warp the heart of a child so that he cannot trust or smile or sing."

" These children all smile and sing and seem to trust," I observed.

" Not all of them — now. But all of them will," he said. " My father prescribes certain medicines — the school and the workshop and the garden, so that they are busy. Idleness is a breeder of this soul sickness. They build and plant and learn. And there is food and clothing and shelter. There are medicines to make them well. But the best medicine is love. Let me tell you about Giglio. But wait. Let us have Giglio for you to see — "

Mr. Fabio threw back his head and called, " Giglio! Giglio! my little brother! " in a voice that shattered the quiet of the garden and seemed to startle even the statues. The buzzing of the saw stopped abruptly in the workshop. The song from the schoolhouse came to an end, and in the stillness that followed we heard soft running footsteps coming from somewhere along one of the paths. A lean, brown youngster, who looked at first to be about six years old, ran around the boxwood hedge. Then up close I saw that he was more probably nine or ten. He was a hunchback. But he appeared not to be conscious of his infirmity, nor to be alarmed at the summons. He looked as if he were delighted to be called.

Fabio put an arm around the hunched shoulders and spoke a few words in Italian. The boy nodded, held out his left hand, then quickly drew it back and presented the right one to me. Fabio patted the shoulders.

" This young man is my secretary," he said. " He loves pencils and paper and some day he will be able to write letters. Now he makes himself essential here by sharpening the pencils. Some day he will understand English, but now he knows only Italian. I have just asked him if I shall tell you about him and he says it will be a good thing."

With the boy standing there quietly confident, Fabio told me Giglio's story.

" Giglio came last November," he said. " After the war he was the only one of his family left alive. There was not even an uncle or a brother left to him. Can you think what it means to be alone? "

He waited, giving me time to think.

" Giglio was forced to beg in the streets for food, and when all from whom he begged were too poor to give, he became a thief. He stole bread and, as he learned the skill, he began to steal money. But all that time Giglio was not a bad boy. It was only that he knew of no other way to stay alive. It required all of my father's medicines to show him the other ways.

" One day he went for an errand to my father's office. My father saw him pick up a red pencil and put it in his pocket, but my father did not speak about it. A little later Giglio returned to the office.

" ' Pastor Santi,' he said to my father. ' We must do some praying at once. A mistake has been made. A boy has stolen a pencil that is your property. Here is the pencil.' "

Fabio stopped again and looked at me earnestly.

" It is a pity you cannot understand Italian," he said. " You should know how my father talks to a boy in trouble. My father said to this one, ' If it were my property it would not be a serious matter, but the pencil does not belong to me. Everything belongs to God, including the pencil.' Then Giglio thought a moment and he said, ' Pastor Santi, *I* was the boy who stole the pencil! ' And my father said to him, ' You cannot steal anything here because it is yours as it is mine, loaned to us both by God. The only difference is that God has asked me to act as steward over what is here. You may have whatever you need. It is helpful if you will speak to me directly when you want it, on account of the responsibility God has placed in me where these things are concerned.' Then he gave the pencil back to Giglio."

" What did Giglio say? " I asked.

" He was glad and he was surprised," Fabio answered. " It was the first time he had realized that one can live and have things without stealing. So then my father said, ' Let us pray and thank God for all his many blessings.' "

Fabio patted the boy's head again and dismissed him with a word in Italian. Then he turned back to me.

" My father has been thanking God in this way for eighty years. And as steward he has a large property in Casa Materna to administer for the Lord."

CHAPTER SIXTEEN

The Story of Casa Materna

Forty-eight years ago Pastor Riccardo Santi, then a young preacher in a Methodist church of Naples, had what he called a Vision. It happened on his birthday when he was out walking, remembering other birthdays, and all the days of his life since his own orphaned childhood, and thinking how he had been unusually blessed in a great many ways. He had a home now, not a very big one to be sure, but clean; and he had a loving wife who looked after him, and two handsome children, as well behaved as the average, and brighter than most, he thought. And he had work that kept his heart glad, because it was in the service of the Lord to whom Pastor Santi had a personal, passionate, and complete devotion. Like most preachers he did not have very much money, but it seemed a miracle of God to have any money at all when he got so much joy and satisfaction from his work.

While thinking these thoughts, and not forgetting to thank God for his blessings, Pastor Santi came upon two poor children, a little boy and his sister who were selling matches on the square.

" Why are you selling matches? " he asked them.

" We sell matches to buy food," the little boy said. " Our mother is sick and our father is dead and there is no money unless we sell matches."

" Do you sell very many? " Pastor Santi asked.

" Alas, Signore," the boy confessed, " we have not sold

three boxes this morning. Every gentleman who passes this corner has no need for matches, it seems."

Then a strange thing happened. Out of the blue sky there seemed to come a Voice.

" Take them and love them for my sake," the Voice said to the young pastor. " As it was done to you, do you also unto these little ones."

Now Pastor Santi believed that the Voice came from God, and he was used to obeying God without asking questions. He took the two children straight home to his wife.

" Who are they? " Signora Santi asked her husband.

" I have not asked their names," he told her. " But they are ours to care for as I was cared for when I was an orphan child."

Now Signora Santi had her household to provide for out of Pastor Santi's small pay. She knew that in his wallet he had only three *lire* that day, and that was all the money there was. There were already two young Santis who were always hungry and wearing out their shoe soles. Furthermore Signora was not so sure about that Voice.

But she was very sure of her husband.

Into their home they took the children that day. They also found a place in the hospital for the children's sick mother, who blessed them for their kindness to her little ones. And when they could not find another home for the children, the Santis kept them as their own.

There wasn't enough room in the house for two more, but Luisa gave the girl her small bed, and Emmanuele gave the boy half of his bed. There wasn't enough food either, which was serious. Luisa gave half her bread and milk every morning to the little girl, and Emmanuele shared his food with the boy. But by Sunday morning there were four hungry children instead of two full ones.

"We have not enough food," the Signora said firmly to her husband. "You will have to do something."

On Sunday morning Pastor Santi used for a sermon text the Bible verse "Inasmuch as ye have done it unto one of the least of these, ye have done it unto me." He told his little congregation in Naples about the children, and about the Voice.

That very afternoon things began to happen. A chair and another bed appeared right out in front of the door of the Santi house. Clothes came — trousers, shirts, dresses and shoes. Potatoes came, and spaghetti and beans. Until late at night the Pastor and the Signora kept going to answer knocks at the door and finding parcels.

"We have too much food!" said the Pastor. "We have more beds than we can use. We can have more children here!"

There were many orphan children in Naples, then as now, and the Santis took another and another and another child into their home until presently there were six children, and then ten, and finally they had to move to a larger house. After a time there were fifty in that second house. They had to move again, into a house that was still not nearly big enough for so large a family, and which had no terrace and no garden, and no place for the children to play. Always Pastor Santi longed for a house with a large space for digging and doing things. "Idleness is a trouble breeder!" he said. But they couldn't get that kind of house. And there was hardly enough money even to keep the one they had.

There was one evening when they had not another loaf of bread in the house, and there was no knowing where breakfast for fifty children would come from. What was worse, there was no money to pay the rent. That was very serious indeed.

" I will sell the living-room couch," said Signora Santi. " It will bring enough money for one meal, and it will pay the rent this month."

" The Lord will provide," said Pastor Santi. " Let us pray before going to the church."

After they had prayed Pastor Santi put on his coat and hat, and started down the dark stairway to the front door to go to his evening church meeting.

" Have no fear," he said to the Signora. " The Lord will provide."

" I hope He will do it rather soon," she said.

Pastor Santi could not see clearly in the dark hallway by the door but he felt someone brush against him, and an envelope was put into his hand.

" Is it a message from one of my people? " he asked. But the dark figure on the stairs went straight on out ahead of him without speaking. By the time Pastor Santi reached the door, there was no one in sight.

He opened the envelope then, and found inside a 2000-*lire* note. Two thousand *lire* were a fortune!

Pastor Santi turned and ran back up the stairs, shouting joyfully.

" Already the Lord has answered the prayer! " he shouted. " There is money for the rent, and for many meals, and you may keep the couch! "

" Who sent the money? " asked the Signora.

" The Lord sent the money," the Pastor said firmly. But looking in the envelope he found a paper which said, " Forgive me." Then he knew that it was his old German army friend Herr Heusch, who hadn't spoken to the Pastor for many weeks.

By this time several years had gone by in that crowded city home, and not many people outside the neighborhood had paid much attention to the Santis' large family of children, except Pastor Santi's loyal little congregation. But one day in 1919 just after the first world war, some visitors came from America. There were five men in a big automobile. They had heard about the orphanage with fifty children in Naples, all jammed together in one city house.

" Frankly," they said to Pastor Santi, " we have come to see how your children live. You seem to be very crowded in this house, Pastor."

" There is more room in the streets than in this house," Pastor Santi agreed. " But I welcome you to take a look around. First look please at the street."

They looked at the street, which was dirty and crowded. The children out there were dirty, and some of them looked sick.

The visitors stayed at the Santi home all of one morning. In the dining room and living room, which during the mornings were converted into schoolrooms, the children crowded closer together to make room for the five big men. In the bedrooms the visitors saw fifty little beds close together, but every one neatly made with its own small blanket and sheet.

" It is better than no bed at all, is it not? " Pastor Santi asked.

At noon they ate the food, the bread, and the spaghetti.

" It is not much but it is better than nothing and it is clean," the Pastor said.

They heard the children singing.

" Only happy children sing," Pastor Santi reminded them. " And only healthy children can sing with such loud voices."

When it was time for them to go, the leader of the visitors spoke.

" We are convinced that you are doing an important job

here," he said. " And we will give you some money for the children. How much do you want? "

" I don't want money," Pastor Santi told them.

" Then what do you want? " they asked.

" I want a new house," he said. " A house with a garden where the children can dig, and a place for a workshop and a school building. And I want a place where they can play ball."

That shocked the visitors because a house big enough to hold all those children, with a garden and a playground be-sides, was quite a large request.

" We will take it under consideration," they said finally. Then they rode away in the big automobile.

When her husband told her about all this, Signora Santi was disappointed.

" Those men will forget! " she exclaimed. " You should have taken the money when they offered it."

" The men may forget, it is true," said Pastor Santi. " But the Lord will not forget."

Days and weeks and finally a month and two months went by, and they heard nothing from the visitors.

" You see, they have forgotten," Signora Santi told her husband. " I was right! "

" The Lord will not forget," Pastor Santi said again. That very day he received three more children whose parents had died far south in Calabria province. These three had walked alone all the long way to Naples. They couldn't be turned away. So now there were fifty-three in the family of children.

At long last, the same big automobile drove up to the door of the Santis' home and the same five men were in it. But only one of them, the leader, got out this time. Pastor Santi invited him to come inside, but he said it was impossible.

" We have come to take you with us to buy a new house for your children," he said.

Pastor Santi didn't stop even to go back to get his hat. He called through the window to tell the Signora that he was going with the men in the automobile to buy a house, and then they started.

They went all over Naples. They looked at every house that was marked for sale. But there was something wrong with every one. Some were too small, some were too dark, some were all right except that they had no room in back for a garden.

Just when they thought they would not find in all Naples exactly the kind of house these children needed, they came to Portici, a poor neighborhood at the edge of the city. There was a big estate which had belonged to the Prince of Monaco many years before. On it was a palace, with a second building right beside the ocean beach where in the old days the Prince and his royal friends used to come to bathe. Between these two buildings was a beautiful garden with palm trees and statues alongside wide smooth paths. It was the most beautiful place in the world for princes — and for children, too.

Pastor Santi looked at the ocean beach and the garden and the two big buildings, one of which was just right for a schoolhouse. He did not say a word.

" How would this do? " the leader asked.

" It is exactly right," said Pastor Santi. " But it is a good deal to ask."

" You shall have it," said the man.

That was more than thirty years ago. The Prince's palace was given a new name, Casa Materna, which means " the motherly house." It was like a dream come true.

As all the years were going by, two more children were

born to the Santis, making four in all. When the time came for them to choose their own places in the world, Emmanuele studied to be a minister like his father. Teofilo studied medicine, because with so many children a doctor would be very much needed. Fabio decided to become a lawyer, because he thought that with such a large family of orphan children living in Casa Materna, his father might need a lawyer's help. And Luisa for many years helped her mother in running the household, and later on she taught school.

Since there were so many more children in Italy without homes and parents, other people started other orphanages. " There are far more homeless children in Naples than Casa Materna can provide for," said Pastor Santi. " If we have encouraged others to help in this big job, then we are pleased. We should have a Casa Materna in every city of Italy."

Then came the second world war. Portici, being down close to the harbor and also near the railway station, was bombed mercilessly.

Those air raids were terrifying times for the leaders of the orphanage, but the children almost enjoyed them. When the siren whistled they were all led into the bomb shelters under the palace. There they sang and sang, at the tops of their voices, " Are we downhearted? No, no, no! " Even though there was never much food to spare, still Signora Santi always saved some bread and jam for these times so that they could have a little party down in the shelter while the bombs whistled over their heads. When the children heard the siren blow, they always thought it meant a party.

This was during the first years of the war. After the bombardments became fiercer, and seven bombs fell right in the garden of Casa Materna, the children were taken out of the castle and sent away from Naples. By that time not only Casa Materna, but the whole of Portici was in ruins. Many people had fled to caves outside the city where they made shift to stay alive. Two years passed before the Santis and the children could return to live in the shambles of the old castle.

The bombs that destroyed Casa Materna were American bombs, but American soldiers helped to rebuild what their air force had destroyed. During the occupation of Italy many soldiers were quartered near the site where Casa Materna's big building had stood by the sea. In their free time the soldiers played with the children, and learned to love them and the Santi family. Several hundred wrote to their friends in America to ask for help for Casa Materna, and at last they raised enough money to help rebuild the schoolhouse and dormitory. Two big visitors' books record the names of these young Americans who had a part in the new life of Casa Materna.

This new life included many children whose parents had been killed in the war and whose homes had been destroyed. A number of them were brought from the caves outside Naples. To every boy and girl who came, alone and bereft, to find refuge at Casa Materna, Pastor Santi would say, " God has provided a place for you, my child, but better than that he has provided a family. Here are your brothers and your sisters. Here is your home."

One boy, Ciro, asked, " Why did God take away my own family? "

Another, Giuseppe, answered quickly, " It was not God that did it. It was the Americans."

" I think it was the fault of the Germans," said Ciro.

Pastor Santi said, " Many German children also are homeless."

Another said, " It was the war."

Another said, " It was the devil."

" Who is right, Pastor? " they asked.

" My children," Pastor Santi reminded them, " these questions are too hard for us. But God is good and this home is his gift to us — to you and to me. We are safe to trust him. That is all I can tell you."

CHAPTER SEVENTEEN

"Life Is O.K."

This is the story, not of the first community center in Italy, but of Angela Buosco, who is housecleaner for the center. I heard it there.

The center is a project planned by Dr. Teofilo Santi, and supported by the Congregational Christian Service Committee of America. It is staffed with two American workers and two Italian workers in residence, and it is located in a fairly new building among the ruins of a section of Naples called Granili. Like Portici, Granili was demolished by bombs during the war, and has hardly been rebuilt at all. It is a crowded section, too, with most of the people herded together in miserable poverty, in dugouts and barracks, and half-destroyed buildings.

The community center provides some schooling, a recreational and crafts program for boys and girls, and a hot lunch. It is one of the few efforts in this area to build up hope and initiative in a spiritually desolate group, as well as to provide some emergency relief in the form of food and clothing.

Angela Buosco, the housecleaner, gave me my first opportunity for a frank talk with an Italian woman whose whole existence was framed out of a need to adjust to the privations of war. These she had converted into opportunities, in her own somewhat unusual way.

I cannot say why Angela attracted me so much. Perhaps it was her personality, which was bumptious and cocky and shrewd. Perhaps it was her independence and good-will. She had certainly been able to take it on the chin, and not to harbor hard feelings either. Perhaps it was her stubborn will to enjoy life to the lees, however it came, and it had come hard. Anyway I would like to make a picture, if I can, of Angela Buosco.

I should begin, I suppose, with the housecleaning. This was badly done, with a gay indifference to inconsequentialities that sang out from the hastily swept floors and from every half-dusted chair that obviously had never been moved for sweeping underneath. But all deficiencies in cleaning were more than made up for by Angela's own bright personality, which affected the whole house.

She spoke some English with a rapid admixture of Italian, interspersed with frequent ejaculations — " O.K." and " You bet " and " Cheerio " — that went along with her casual housekeeping, and kept fooling me into thinking I was understanding what she said.

She was a typical southern Italian in appearance, with a thin brown face, black eyes that sparkled and blazed, sometimes with indignation or wrath, more often with humor, of which she had more than her share. Her coal-black hair would have been beautiful if it had had a recent wash, or even contact with a comb or a brush. But it hung to her shoulders, careless like the rest of her. There were also a certain straightforwardness and a sly impudence about her that were refreshing.

She was all eagerness to tell me everything, and more than I wanted to know.

" Italy? War? Refugees? " She knew everything about them, all there was to know, including all about soldiers, and she would be delighted to tell me. She would even take the whole job over and write the story herself, except that she could not write English at all, and only a little Italian. She had three children, and she wanted to take me to where she lived, so I could see " that hell-hole."

I was overwhelmed by such enthusiasm, which disposed of any need for tact or delicacy. Here was someone who was ready and eager to get down to brass tacks. I put on my coat and hat and got ready to start to Granili barracks, where she lived.

" After the return, then the cleaning! " she said without concern. Obviously the literary was far more essential than the domestic. We left the cleaning merrily to go to pot.

Our way led first through several grim streets, where all the buildings were in ruins, over a streetcar track that picked its way among debris, and past two whole city blocks that were only piles of refuse. What walls were left standing, although of stone, looked as if a strong wind off the Mediterranean might collapse them completely. Window openings gaped, holes without glass, some without frames. And yet in most of these places families lived, and swinging across the streets, from window to high window, were the clotheslines strung with tattered clothing. Down in the street were swarms of dirty children, some nearly naked. To make things even more desolate, it began to rain before we had half covered the distance to Granili, and by the time we had reached the huge stone barracks where Angela lived, rain was coming down heavily.

The barracks building is called Granili, like the section of town. Originally it must have been quite an imposing structure, for it had, Angela told me, housed a big division of Mussolini's soldiers.

" And, by the way," she said (" by the way " was another of those deceptive phrases she used), " You all thought we

were great for Mussolini." There followed a flood of Italian
mixed with a little English, and she gave me to understand
that that was a mistake, or at least that Angela Buosco herself had never liked Mussolini. He gave them jobs, and they
liked that. Everybody had a job in Italy when Mussolini
was here. But when he wanted their wedding rings, they
didn't like that. " I bet you saw pictures of the people throw-
ing away their wedding rings," she said. " They not want to.
They got to. That was how."

I looked at the barracks with respect, although now it was
a ruin, with a good part of the roof blown off and more falling away. It occupied what would have been about half a
city block, and had three floors. Angela told me there were
5,000 people living there.

Before we went in, she gave me instructions on how to be-
have. I must keep close to her, must not get out of her sight,
must keep quiet and try not to talk, especially English. When
I asked if people objected to Americans here, she replied that
it wasn't that. But all Americans were supposed to be rich,
and I might be robbed. She thought it would be a good idea
for me not to carry money in my pocketbook, if I had any
money, because it was better not to have anything " loose."
I put my passport and coin purse inside my coat and trudged
along close behind her, wondering what was to come next.

Just then two children came from somewhere outside to
join us, and, as we went in through the great archway which
was the door, another child, a girl about twelve, came along
carrying a young baby which Angela grabbed and hugged
affectionately.

" Mine! " she exclaimed, and encircled all four in her
arms. " All mine! "

The children were very different in appearance. The baby,

about six months old, was dark like her mother. Another, about four, was pure blonde. This one Angela pulled out from behind her skirts where the child clung shyly, and showed her to me proudly. " Papa is American soldier! " she declared. The third was dark, but not so dark as the baby.

We entered the building then, going through the great archway into a long dark arcade, which looked like the covered markets of Istanbul, except that there was nothing here to buy. On either side, straight along to the end, there were high doorways, one after the other. Angela told me that behind each door lived a family. Some families were large, some small. One door was open, and inside I saw what looked like seven or eight toilets and a row of wash bowls. I gathered from Angela that this was the only water closet in the building, and later found that it was true. One bathroom for 5000 people!

The arcade was so dark for most of the way that I kept stumbling over the cobblestones. Angela took my arm and guided me, but a little impatiently, and as though she thought any idiot should be able to walk on her own feet. When occasionally we passed an open door lending a little light to the passageway, I saw that we were not the only ones in the arcade. A good many people sat on the floor against the walls, and once in a while I could distinguish low talking. But not very much. I didn't need my instructions about keeping close to Angela.

Her home, one room, was at the far end of the arcade. The floor inside the room was made of cobblestones, and the walls also were of stone, about twenty feet high. The only light came from a small opening at the top, which was far too high of course for anybody to look out through. The place was cold and I shivered.

" Don't you have a stove in here? " I asked her. She looked amazed.

" Stove? " she asked. " What for a stove? There is never a stove in this house."

" Not even in winter? " I asked.

" But why? It is never freeze in Italy! It is damp, but it is never freeze." Apparently the cold was no problem.

The crowded quarters did not worry her either. There were three beds in the room, one cot-sized, the other two more like little bunks. She told me that there were living in that room her mother, a sister whose husband had left her, and her sister's child, as well as herself and her own three children.

" Sister's man vamoose! That is the way with soldiers! " she told me disdainfully. " Me — I no marry the soldier! " Then she laughed. " I like him though! "

The room was large, but I thought a family of seven was quite a crowd. Again she indicated that she didn't mind being crowded. What she did mind was the fact that this place had formerly been a stable for horses.

There were traces of tears in her black eyes when she told me, " Human beings and horses should not live in same place."

But she had made it as cheerful as she could, and got rid of the stable atmosphere rather successfully. For one thing all the walls were whitewashed with lime. For cooking there was a small charcoal stove — although, she said, " There is not much to cook! "

Prominent in the big bare stable room, and fitting well against the religious whiteness of the walls, was the crucifix set up in a corner, with fresh flowers placed before it. I knew they had been bought for a *lira* or two on the corner. She was proud of that crucifix, and kept me standing in front of it for several minutes, while she talked, in that bewildering mixed speech which now was becoming rather familiar. It was comprehensible enough at any rate to make me feel pretty sure that I was understanding what seemed to be Angela's philosophy of life.

" The Holy Virgin! " she murmured. " Jesu Bambino! She is good. My babies pray every morning. No pray, no eat. My mother pray. My sister good. My sister pray. I have sins. I tell priest, no good. I tell Holy Virgin. I feel good. It is bad, that hell. Maybe like a stable.

" Long time ago I know Angela get it hard. For some people things go easy. For me, hard. No money. The mother, the sister, the babies. The mother always cry, ' Ah, I hate Americans that bomb house! ' The sister always cry, ' Ah, I hate the husband that take another woman.' They all cry, ' I hate stable to live. It is not enough beds. No good.'

" Me, I say it is no good crying. It is all done. House is bombed. It is gone, goodbye. The husband it is gone, good-bye man! So there is a stable. All right, so we take it. There is other men. All right, so they pay money. Sure it is a sin. I tell Virgin and feel good. I no go to hell. Now I got job of cleaning the house. That is good. Life is good, anyhow. Life is O.K.! "

She beamed, suddenly, and so brightly that the whole stable looked lighter. Then she adjusted the flowers in the vase under the crucifix, and finally reached up to pat the cross affectionately.

" Life is O.K.," she repeated.

Abruptly we were done with deeper things.

" You see enough? " she inquired. I had. " We go back for the business."

She took the baby in her arms, told the children to come along, and the whole caravan of us made the long trek back through the arcade, into the dreary streets, and past all the

ruins to the community center. There she threw off her raincoat and picked up the mop. There was some indifferent
swishing, after that, but chiefly the mop was used for gestures,
while she continued her story. This went along so rapidly
that there was no chance for questions, because Angela
seemed to have her own ideas about it, and I had all I could
do to keep up with her talk, and try to guess sometimes what
she was telling me.

We were interrupted only when she stopped for breath and
went at the mopping vigorously for a moment, or when now
and again the children came in to be talked to, ever so lovingly, or when the baby had an unexpected requirement of
nature, and had to be lifted off the couch and held up over the
floor, and the puddle wiped up afterward. The drama was
furnished by the gestures, and by Angela's eyes, which blazed
and sparkled dangerously sometimes, and sometimes merrily.

When the war with America came home to them, Angela
was living with her mother and her sister and her sister's
husband, the one who later " vamoosed," in a flat some distance from Portici. She gestured scornfully with the mop
in the direction of the bleak street outside, giving me to understand that she herself did not really belong to Portici. The
first bombing by the Americans happened in August 1943.
The family ran to an air-raid shelter, where they stayed all
night.

" It was long, that night! " she remarked reminiscently.
" Many people close up together."

The next day they went back to the house. " But there was
not a house! " she exclaimed. " The house in little bits."

I interrupted to ask how she felt about the Americans, and
she replied, Yankee-fashion, with a question.

" What *you* think about people that made your house in
little bits? " she asked.

They tried to get a room in a hotel, but the hotels left standing were already crowded with people like themselves who had been bombed out. They " slept out " at night, which wasn't too bad in August, but later on when winter came it was very bad. They came to Portici then, and lived with other families, first one and then another, until these places too were destroyed.

" Then all over bombed! " she said. " Just like you see. It was bad, the fire, and the boom, and people running! "

For a long time they had no roof again. They slept anywhere they could.

" For *me*, well — " she made several eloquent gestures. " What you think? " she asked me.

After the American soldiers came, Angela noticed that they were kind to the children and gave them candy.

" The Germans they take the candy from baby! " She laughed delightedly at her own joke.

She began to like the American soldiers. She found a room to live in (perhaps the one at the Granili barracks, although I was not sure about that) and had soldiers there all the time. They were good soldiers, she said. Plenty money. And plenty good. At this point she reached for the blonde child, who was standing by her chair, hugged her passionately and then pushed her away, and went on mopping.

She mopped in silence for a little while.

" So now you see. I got the job," she said. " Story is done."

The cleaning apparently also was done, for she put the mop in the corner, gathered her brood of three, wrapped her own coat around two of them and a scarf around the baby, kissed them all, and started back to Granili barracks, in the rain.

From outside the door, she called back — " Cheerio! "

FROM FRANCE

CHAPTER EIGHTEEN

Exiles From Spain

Spain's civil war (1936–1939) engaged the imaginations and idealism of many people in the United States even though most of us knew very little about what was going on. We did know that the centuries-old Spanish monarchy had been replaced by a republican form of government, and that the young republic had been attacked by General Franco and his army. A good deal of romantic literature was written around it, and some of the young men of our country went to Spain to fight with the Loyalist Republicans against Franco's Falangists. The revolution ended in 1939, with Franco's army the victors. The newspapers stopped talking about Spain, and headlines began reporting the second world war.

Today tourists travel in Spain with complete ease and are thrilled with the historic beauty, the friendliness and comfort they find there. Vegetable markets in the cities overflow with strange attractive fruits and vegetables. Craftsmen offer for sale their hand-tooled metals, their delicate baskets, charming clay jugs and pots. The skies are blue, birds sing, and all seems serenity and beauty. Franco's government is recognized by other nations, and the revolution is as forgotten in world politics as though it had never happened.

As always, the ones who lost the war are those who remember. Some who are still Loyalist Republicans keep in hiding, exiles in their own country, silent with their memories. There are also the exiles who escaped with the Republican army and fled across the Pyrenees to France.

On the boat on my way back to New York from the Mediterranean I met Ovideo, one of the Loyalists who remained in Spain.

Ovideo was young, quiet at first, then more talkative as he gained confidence among the cosmopolitan group of free talkers about him — Italians, a large crowd of Arab students, Jews returning from a Zionist conference in Israel, and emigrés from a score of countries seeking asylum in America. Ovideo liked the opportunity of practicing his English, which was slow but correct.

He told me that he had been trying for a long time to get a visa to the United States. Of course only the recent rather circumspect diplomatic friendship between his country and ours had made this possible. He could scarcely believe even now that he had been so lucky. I had the impression that every string in his home town of Barcelona had been pulled, and that half of Spain must have had a share in getting all his papers signed and the red tape unwound.

" But now I go! " he exclaimed. " Now I can live! And I have some years to live, because I am a young man still."

" Do you expect to make a lot of money in America? " I asked curiously.

" I do not know," he said. " Perhaps. I learn that it is very costly to live there. But I want to escape from prison. My father was a Loyalist. He is dead."

" Why do you talk about prison? " I asked. " The civil war was over twelve years ago at least."

" It was ended," he said. " But it will never be over for the people who lost in the war. And for their children. We are prisoners. I am very lucky because I have the friendship of certain very important people. I am very lucky."

He was reluctant to talk about the revolution, which he remembered well. " We do not speak of it," he said. " There is no use. It is better not to say anything — for the people who lost."

" Do you think there will be another civil war in Spain? " I asked.

" I do not think so," he said. " Some think so. But for me — well, it is over. We make the best of things. The trouble with war is that you might not win. Even if your side is just. Even if you sacrifice everything. Still you might not win because war is won by weapons, not by principles."

" Then you feel hopeless — as if your ' side ' would always be prisoners of tyranny? " I asked.

" Hopeless for me, perhaps for my children," he said. " But not forever. There may be another revolution. I do not think the Republic could win. But a change of heart and mind in the present government, that is possible sometime. This is because our conquerors are Spanish people, even though they fought us who are also Spanish people. The Spanish people are one race and they cannot always be divided. It will come slowly. But it is possible."

I wondered why he should be determined to leave his country which with the next century might see a new order created. Ovideo was quick to defend himself. He said that he himself was only one, that he was the exception because only one in many thousand would be lucky enough to go to America, and that for everyone who could it was the thing to do. But he admitted a certain prejudice against the large group who had escaped years ago across the mountains to France.

" I and my family stayed to suffer the fate of the vanquished," he said. " But I do not think those others who fled to France are well off there. A half-million! They are a lost colony."

Ovideo is most likely doing all right for himself in America. Besides being lucky, as he said, he is also unusually intelligent. I fancy he will quickly find his way to a group of intellectuals and will be accepted.

But what of the half-million republicans who fled across the Pyrenees into France? When Germany occupied France in 1941, these Spanish republicans again became refugees, and thousands have spent years in French internment camps. Many were deported to Germany or put in labor camps. What they suffered in privation and deliberate mistreatment at the hands of the Germans is not fully known.

When the war ended, many escaped from concentration camps in Germany and from labor camps in France, but they were still unable to return to their homeland. In the meantime France, overflowing with refugees from other European countries, as well as with her own thousands of homeless people, could not provide adequately for these Spanish refugees. They stayed on because there was no place for them to go, but they stayed in poverty, crowded into inadequate quarters and without sufficient food.

There is not room here to go into the various divisions among the Spanish refugees, which had to do largely with the different times of their escape or deportation from Spain. Some of them were resettled in the United States and Canada and South America through the International Refugee Organization. Some, not classified as political refugees, had no help from IRO; and, since IRO ended in 1950, none of them have had any help from that source.

During this time, of course, a great many children have been born and have grown up in a crowded and unwholesome way of living, themselves making more mouths to feed. The French government has provided some social security and some assistance. Some agencies have donated food and clothing. But as to being able to live independently, to make a living, to look forward to any kind of satisfying future — there is nothing.

Some hundreds of these destitute Spanish refugees live in the city of Toulouse in shacks built on the damp and unhealthy flats beside the river. After nearly ten years of wars of one kind and another, and through seven years of nervous peace, these refugees still live apart from the French. Children have been born there who have never known what it is to be clothed, adequately fed, and healthy. Many are delicate, and a large percentage predisposed to tuberculosis.

At St. Goin, a tiny village in the foothills of the Pyrenees, about fifty miles from Toulouse, the Unitarian Service Committee has for a number of years operated a nursing home for some of these children.

It was to this home that I went to meet the Spanish children, to try to understand some of their special and poignant problems.

CHAPTER NINETEEN

Children of the Pyrenees

Six dreary hours in the crowded, cold, and rainy city of Toulouse were enough to make the village of St. Goin seem like a little piece of heaven to me, when I finally got there. It wasn't strange at all to hear of Manuel, aged nine, who had waited by his father's mailbox in the city day after day, hoping that this day or the next he would find in the mail a " big envelope " which would be his acceptance into the St. Goin Home.

The journey to the village was beautiful, too. Short moments after leaving Toulouse (in a gray drizzle) our train moved swiftly into sunswept farming country, then more gradually into rolling hills, and finally into the *montagnes*, which all the passengers in my compartment waited eagerly to see. Especially they waited and watched for Lourdes, and the grotto shrine where Bernadette had seen her vision. " You are lucky! " they assured me earnestly. " From this very window you shall see that sacred spot! "

When we reached Lourdes at last they all fell silent, crossed themselves reverently, and whispered in low tones. Always, they said, there was the chance — the barest small chance — that some person who had been cured by the saint would climb up on the train and tell how he had thrown his crutches into the grotto. But no such person came to us on this occasion, and presently we started on again, to Pau.

At Pau I left the train, and went on by car to St. Goin,

which is too small a village for any train. One might not even know that it is a village except for the wee inn with its neat small sign over the low door.

I stayed at night at the inn and during the day at the St. Goin Home with the children. The two places had nothing in common except that the inn furnished a charming frame of local color, complete with outside plumbing, and chickens and pigs walking about under my casement window. Nights were enchanting because often the villagers would gather in the coffee room just underneath my bedroom, to sing folk-songs. When I gave up and went to sleep they were some-times still harmonizing down there.

When something was needed, I rapped on the floor with the heel of my shoe, whereupon Madame, a rosy, cheerful young woman, came rushing up the narrow stairs with a pitcher of hot water, or whatever was required. I slept un-der an enormous feather puff, and in the morning was wakened with a tray of *petit déjeûner — café au lait* in a grandfather-sized cup, and two halves of a loaf of French bread, spread half an inch thick with butter.

Madame and I then had a spirited little conversation in which I tried out all the French words I knew, she tried hard to understand and to answer appropriately, and we both did a good deal of gesturing and smiling. Sometimes between gestures and mixed French we talked about the Spanish refugees. She was acquainted with the Home where I went each day, and spoke with great sympathy of *les pauvres en-fants*.

Then, all waked up with coffee, I opened the shutters and looked down to the little courtyard below where usually there were several curious children and some grown-ups standing among the chickens, looking up at my window.

The early morning walk down a country road, disclosing

new pictures at every turning, was always brisk and pleasant, with the bright sun and dark clouds hastening after each other in quick succession. It was hardly ever warm outdoors. And it was *never* warm inside the building which was the children's home.

The great front gates were a little too big, and a little too grim, and seemed to separate the children inside from the countryside outside. Although I probably imagined all this, it went along with other feelings I learned to have about the Spanish children in France, for always, as I saw them playing and working and studying, they seemed to me set apart. They were *in* this country, but not really *of* it.

The building was one of the vast, cold palaces one sees so often in Europe, with enormous rooms, high ceilings, and great shadowy hallways. To me they seemed dismal. But then I did not have the damp and crowded slums of Toulouse with which to compare them. And it was soon apparent that however cheerless all this might look to an American visitor, it was a real home for thirty Spanish children. They were warm enough in cotton dresses and jeans.

I learned that the children came there for three-month periods, continuing their schoolwork along with a treatment of rest and food which was meant to build up their bodies and refuel their spirits for enduring the slums they would return to. Of course the bad food and close damp quarters in Toulouse were likely to undo the work of St. Goin, so that often they returned for a second period, or a third, of rebuilding bodies. But the wholesome effect on their spirits I thought must surely be something that could not be lost.

I spent hour after quiet hour under a big tree in the front yard, close to the playground, trying to catch whatever warmth there was in occasional flashes of sunlight, while the younger children played near by. It was a useful, anonymous way of studying and thinking about them. We talked very little, partly because of the language barrier, and partly because there seemed to be no need of talking.

Walkyrie, Henrique, Carmen, Luisa, Dolores, Manuel — dark and fair, not striking or unusual as individuals, they were altogether, in a group, beautiful and for some reason very touching children. They were oddly independent, more than usually on their own, it seemed to me. They were not shy, but neither were they curious or concerned. I was charmed by their complete indifference to me as a person and a stranger. When now and again a doll or a ball or a straw hat (once it was some kind of bug in a glass bottle) was tossed casually into my lap, and later retrieved by the owner without a word or a glance my way, I felt comfortably like an empty chair or a table top. There was some sort of acceptance there, I thought. But so was everything accepted. So was everybody accepted. So was life itself accepted, apparently.

These were the things I thought as I sat there, and one by one the children began to live for me out of their backgrounds and home life. And as I discovered this same curious independence in so many of their actions all day long, I felt that the early impressions had not been entirely wrong. Certainly they were not like the intense and eager Italian children. Certainly they were not dramatic like the Arabs, warm like the Greeks, or wise and shrewd like the Turkish youngsters I had known. Certainly they were not like any American children I have known, even those silent individualists of the southern mountains.

I tried to think what the difference might be. They were like children, and yet not childlike. I wondered if this odd, removed way they had were a Spanish characteristic, or if it were a quality that came from being Spanish in France — rootless without even knowing it was so. I am still wonder-

ing, and I'm not sure that the rest of this story gives a direction for thinking, but I believe it may be pertinent.

There was Walkyrie, for instance — Walkyrie, with her
doll. As I watched her, and thought about Toulouse and the
family she belonged to, I wondered what the future might
hold for this little girl. I'm sure Walkyrie was not wondering! She was perhaps ten years old, an age when children
do wonder. She was plump and blonde with protruding blue
eyes and a rather blank expression, altogether not especially
bright or attractive, but sweet and kind, and an enthusiastic
eater. Her father had died about the time she was born,
while he was in forced labor in Germany during the occupation. Her mother had worked as a weaver in Toulouse until
a year or two before, when she had succumbed to a severe
nervous depression. These were the cold facts. And here
was Walkyrie playing cheerfully in a garden in France, where
she was not, and probably would never be, a citizen. Walkyrie played with her doll. I was depressed.

There was Manuel, now eleven. He was the boy who
waited for the mailman when he was nine. Manuel had two
younger brothers in Toulouse, Jean Claude, five, and Alain,
two. This Manuel was large for his age and plain, but there
was an air he had of managing the playground which gave
me hope for him. When the war with Franco broke out,
Manuel's father had just passed his examination as a regular officer of the Republican army in Spain. He had fled to
France in 1939 to be interned by the Germans in various
camps until the end of World War II. During his internment
this man's body was " experimented " on by the Germans.
After the liberation he had been fortunate enough to obtain
an apprenticeship in typography and then employment in a
printshop, although he can never work regularly because his
health was ruined during the internments. Manuel had al-

ways been a delicate though large child, and his health had suffered from living with the whole family in one small room of a damp slum house down by the river in Toulouse. I wondered about Manuel. He lined up six of the younger children in front of him, gave a curt command in French, and they went marching off across the playground. It was encouraging.

There was Dolores, whom I thought quite beautiful. She was half-Spanish and half-Moorish, dark with bright apple cheeks and a dazzling smile. Dolores' mother had been a goosegirl in Spain before the civil war, and this little girl had spent many of the hours of her short life alone on the hillsides, keeping sheep there in the Spanish Pyrenees. The two had fled to France because her mother hoped to find a place where Dolores might go to school. But she was no scholar, I could see. I wondered if the streets of Toulouse had anything for Dolores that was better than a Spanish hillside. I wondered what the long hours alone in the hills, sometimes all night, had meant to her, and what she thought about then and now. It was possible that she had not thought at all. She seemed quite untouched by what went on about her, and by people, even the other children. Alone, in the swing, she pushed with her feet on the ground, and went higher and higher.

There were all the others, not so unusual, not too attractive, but in a group somehow complete, and separate. As I watched them there, and later in the dining room, and in the big cold dormitories where they took their naps and slept at night, I tried to think how life must seem to them, and how they would perhaps face it later. I couldn't find an answer which satisfied me.

One thing which surprised me about them was the stoicism — or perhaps it was fortitude — that they showed. They seemed not to complain about anything. They did not beg.

It is seldom one sees a group of children with so little apparent demand for attention. This was especially surprising since most of them must have had, fundamentally, a great need for love and security. They seemed to show a sort of fatalism, an attitude of what-is-to-be-will-be. There was an incident which happened on an automobile ride we had with five of them one afternoon which illustrates this.

The ride was beautiful, over rolling hills and through green planted valleys, sunny and enchanting, and the children enjoyed it with their habitual calm ecstasy. On the way back the engine moaned and stopped, and it appeared that the gas was bad. We had to wait on the road while an accommodating passer-by in a small auto went on to the next town and telephoned someone at the home to come and fetch us.

While we were waiting, not sure that this passer-by would carry the message, we walked with the children around over the paths nearby and up the road. They were deeply interested in our plight and more concerned than they appeared to be. Little Carmen, a delightful four-year-old with big warm eyes, was most serious about the whole business. She took my hand and walked me up and down for a while and chattered continuously in what I took to be French baby-talk. One remark I understood and remembered. " After all it would have been better if we had taken a bicycle. This couldn't have happened with a bicycle, never! "

Presently she ventured to ask if it were probable that we would *marcher* all the way home. I thought we might have to *marcher* to the next town, which was a good six miles away, and not too much fun to think about, but we tried to make light of the matter. Carmen thought it over and said not one single other word.

In the meantime the three boys had gone down to play in

the creek. Henrique, who had brought along a toy windmill (a gift from a recent Canadian Unitarian box), carried it down to the water. But amid all the excitement of digging for worms and making mud houses, he laid his windmill on the bank and forgot it. After a while they returned to the car, the windmill still forgotten.

Half an hour later while we were still waiting in the car, Henrique uttered the briefest little panic-stricken exclamation. We followed his gesture, looked down at the creek, and there saw a little girl, a stranger from a nearby farmhouse, holding the windmill.

I looked at Henrique and the whole tragic story of the civil war was written in his eyes. He looked at the windmill, made one move to leap from the car and run down to claim it, stopped, shrugged his shoulders, and silently settled down in his seat. He might as well have said, " C'est fini! "

That's what I mean by the fatalism or the stoicism or the fortitude which I felt in the Spanish children.

Meals were unexpectedly cheerful occasions. My seat faced the table where the seven smallest girls, including Walkyrie, had their places. These were the ones without appetites, except for Walkyrie, who ate with gusto, and no doubt had been put there to encourage the others by example. There was one among them, Luisa, who resembled a saint of the middle ages, with two raven black braids, delicate carved features, and soft, mild eyes (her two missing front teeth added a piquant touch). On one triumphant day Luisa was the winner of the prize known as " Christmas " for finishing her bowl of porridge first. " Christmas " meant the opportunity to choose one each from the stack of used Christmas cards kept on the shelf at a corner of the dining room. Most times Walkyrie was the winner of " Christmas."

One morning when I went over from the inn, I found all

the children in great excitement getting dressed up in their Basque costumes to give an exhibition of Basque folk dances. They were sweet and pretty in their long red skirts and black Basque waists and white kerchiefs. They went through the intricate figures of the folk dances so skillfully and with such abandon that it was heart-touching. It was as though something in them said that this was their moment — these short three months in all their lives were to be enjoyed as children enjoy things, completely, and without reckoning that they will cease to be, that they must have an end. And so they danced without a cloud to mar their joy.

Something of all this I tried to say to Dr. Penal, the Spanish doctor for the Home, when I talked with him after dinner. Dr. Penal told me that he, like the children, was a refugee from Spain, an escapee with the Republican army across the Pyrenees. He had left his wife and three children in Spain and had not seen them for seventeen years.

" Often I wonder," he said, " how they are growing there and what is happening to them. Once in a while I hear, but only that they are alive. That is all."

Dr. Penal knew well the records of the children which I had been reading. When I remarked on how much the same they were, he nodded his understanding.

" You mean the circumstances of their parents' escape, their privations here, the experiences in the labor camps? "

" And the mental breakdown of so many of the parents," I supplied. " Is it because they are worn out with suffering? "

" I suppose it is because they have lost any reason for hoping," he said. " So long as there was a reason to fight and a reason to hope for something they could stay healthy in their minds. As long as one can fight the mind is secure."

I spoke of the irony of the unconsciousness of the children as they played in the garden. Nothing of what would happen to them was their responsibility, and yet it would become their responsibility. I spoke of the poignant abandon of the dancing, the fortitude of Henrique about the windmill, and said that out of all these things I had read and seen, I was trying to understand the Spanish children. He nodded again as if trying to follow my meaning. I asked what he thought the war had made of them, whether they knew it or would ever know it.

Dr. Penal said that he himself was a student of child psychology and a disciple of Anna Freud, and he knew that the Spanish children had been less hurt psychologically by the war than German and French children who had been through similar experiences.

" It is because our people have been conditioned by generation after generation of war," he said. " Now their problems are not so much the effects of suffering on their minds as the practical results, the economic results war has made for them. If economic circumstances can be adjusted to favor them, they will be all right. It will all be as nothing, the horrors they have seen, because they are prepared for them in the experience of the race."

" Does that mean that you think a history of war has strengthened them? " I asked. He repeated that Spanish history has so conditioned Spanish people that they can adjust themselves to war or to whatever comes " bravely." " What they have endured will keep them strong, the Spanish! " he assured me.

Seeing that he didn't quite understand what I was getting at, I tried to make the question clearer.

" You think then that the fortitude built up by such conditioning justified the war by which they were conditioned? Can't we visualize a fortitude and courage which might be built up without violence? "

He seemed bewildered.

" We have always had wars," he said at last. " Perhaps we do not know how to live without them. We have fought other nations bravely. We have fought even against each other. We do not worry about it until the time comes. Then we fight bravely."

" But what is to become of these children? " I asked. " Is there no situation in life for which this ' conditioning ' prepares them except to fight bravely if necessary? Is there no plan for them? "

" We do not plan," he admitted. " We do not wish for war. Only if there should be, I and the Spanish will know how to meet it. We cannot look ahead. We take what comes as it comes. Five years — ten years — we do not look ahead."

I saw the children playing joyously in the garden. They were not looking ahead. But I asked Dr. Penal if he could dream ahead — five years, ten years, and tell me what he thought the future might hold for the children.

" Well," he said in some bewilderment, " life will be harder for them when they grow up. They will be unable to get jobs or to go to higher schools, because they are not French."

" Is there no movement, no agency, no party which will help them to grow into independent, self-respecting citizens? " I persisted.

He said there was not, so far as he knew, and there was no use to plan, because they could not be citizens until they were eighteen and decided for themselves whether or not to be French citizens.

" Will this uncertainty as to who they really are, what they will be — will this have an effect on them? " I asked. " Will it make them unstable and irresponsible as adults? "

" Perhaps — perhaps not," he said, as if it really didn't matter. " They are Spanish, and they will take what comes. You Americans can hardly understand the Spanish because your country is so young. It has not yet been made. You yourselves have not been made. But the Spanish character is a finished character. It is not of individuals but of the race. You cannot change a Spaniard. That is why we cannot understand each other on the subject of war. We accept it along with all that comes because war always comes. The individual now — this ten years — it does not matter. The years are gone, the individual is dead. Time goes fast. We are all dead. What does it matter? "

" I believe it matters," I said.

" You are an American," he said smiling, and I understood the discussion was over.

Carmen came running up with half a chain of clovers she had made, and held it in one hand while she reached for the doctor's ear with the other, and whispered to him. I caught the word *chapeau.*

" She would like a straw hat like Henrique's," he explained. " I have told her that straw hats are for boys. The girls must be content with bonnets."

" But why? "

He smiled again. " I do not know why. It is only that it is so."

FROM GERMANY

CHAPTER TWENTY

The German Problem

In order to study the problems of postwar Germany, as they relate to individuals whose lives have been " affected or redirected as a result of war," one must consider the individual citizens of the country. He must consider also the more than 12,000,000 refugees, expelled or escaped from any of a dozen countries outside the borders of present-day Germany. It is a study which requires a deeper capacity for insight and understanding than perhaps anyone is able to achieve. But we dare not ignore these people and their problems.

Under the guidance of officials of the Lutheran World Federation in Frankfurt, Hamburg, and Berlin, I saw refugee families in camps and barracks and crowded " bunkers." I talked with hundreds of people, and met hundreds of other I couldn't talk to because they came from countries whose languages even a German interpreter couldn't translate for me. I saw how they live, felt something of their losses, and came to know some of them personally.

Such an experience leaves one with the defeated feeling of having been given a responsibility which he cannot begin to meet, and with a great longing to lay at the feet of all who will look and listen the whole of what he has seen. And yet one is stifled with the impact of so many brief poignant pictures passing before his eyes and heart, like fast-moving dreams, not fixed to any background that he knows, with no past, and no future that he can bear to see.

The Latvian family in a Hamburg barracks, father and mother and two big handsome boys slowly dying with tuberculosis, yet working industriously at little craft jobs to earn a little money, and keep busy.

The schoolboy who had been forced to flee to Berlin from Czechoslovakia because, as he told me, he wrote for his lesson, " I do not know *who* started the Korean war."

The piles of rubble in the streets of Mainz where little wisps of smoke indicated that this ruin was a home.

The withered funeral wreath hanging over a heap of broken stone that might once have been a house, with people.

The wooden cross in front of the heap, chalked " *Mutter*."

The " Bahnhof Missions " in Berlin crowded with new arrivals, carrying all they owned in cardboard boxes or bags. The weary, hopeless crowds lounging in the small entrance ways of the bunkers, waiting — and waiting.

Every German I knew was a story of what war does to people. Many of them were not, technically, refugees. Only two of the stories related here have come from a refugee settlement. The Lithuanian group in Diepholz is one tiny part of the great picture of multitudes of shifting people, encamped in a permanently transient state, without roots, without security, without loyalties, in a land foreign to them.

The " brown babies " of Germany, who are told about here, are not refugees in the usual sense of the word — that is, they were not born outside of Germany. But they are individuals whom war has brought to the world, and with problems which are peculiar, and of importance to American people, inasmuch as the fathers of these children are Americans.

The stories told here have two virtues. They happened and are happening. And they are richly indicative of the thousands and millions of true stories of people which are not told here or anywhere.

CHAPTER TWENTY-ONE

Half-and-Half: the "Brown Babies"

The following record is of Giessen, the "brown babies," and Kathy Prugel. It is neither official nor objective, because Kathy Prugel is not objective about the problem, and Kathy has given deeper than official love to the brown children of Germany. Nor can I be objective myself after having seen Giessen with my own eyes, and having watched Kathy with her children. Here is the story.

When I went to the Unitarian Service Committee's headquarters in Boston to ask advice about where to go to find the "brown babies," they suggested that I hunt for a certain Mrs. Kathy Prugel who ran a settlement or a service center or an orphanage of some kind, called "Haven of Hope," in Giessen. This Haven of Hope, they understood, was especially concerned with the children of German women and Negro soldiers, and the Unitarian Service Committee had sent many boxes of clothing to the place.

That was about all they could tell me. I wrote a letter to Mrs. Prugel, addressed to the Haven of Hope in Giessen, Germany, and then went on my way. Three months later in Frankfurt, I wrote again — although, by that time, having heard nothing from Giessen, I had about made up my mind that neither Mrs. Prugel nor her Haven of Hope really existed. It was something like receiving a surprise package from home, therefore, to have a handwritten postcard three days later, saying, " I will meet your train on Saturday morn-

ing and show you my children." It was signed simply
" Kathy."

She met me at the railroad station, a small, blonde, gay,
warm girl, looking younger than she probably was, and wearing a black raincoat instead of a topper on that sunny, frigid
day. She spoke — or rather poured out — a fluent American kind of English that was bright with colloquialisms and
slang. I felt at home with her immediately.

She met me without a car, which indicated that whoever
Kathy Prugel might be, she was certainly no United Nations
official. She did not speak of her position or her job or her
Haven of Hope, and for some reason I hesitated to bring up
the subject.

" You want to get right to work! " she said to me at once.
" All right. Let us then visit the ' brown babies '! "

Without further formalities we started straight from the
station out into the overwhelming city of Giessen.

Riding on a streetcar, or in an automobile, no city seems
too alarming. But walking gives a different viewpoint. I
kept hesitating at the broad traffic intersections, and Kathy
kept dragging me firmly into the midst of the jam and clatter.
She said, " You aren't crossing streets much, I guess! "

It was not very far to the back alley where we found the
first of the children. This one lived with her mother in an
upstairs room. The little girl, a pretty youngster with curly
hair and black eyes, talked to Kathy from the window just
over our heads. I understand that the mother had gone out
and locked the door behind her so that the child couldn't
get out.

" She has had a bad time at the school," Kathy told me.
" This is the first year for any of the Negro children to attend
school, and they have been mistreated here in Giessen. It is
not so bad in Frankfurt and in Munich, but it is very bad in

Giessen. That is why her mother locks the door. Well, better luck next time! "

Again we started out through the Giessen streets. Since it was not a school day there were many children playing in the streets. Even if I had been a casual observer, which I was not, I would have noticed the large number of dark children, contrasting sharply with the decidedly blonde German youngsters.

" There are so many," Kathy told me. " And here sometimes you see the white and colored playing together. In the schools it is different, I am sorry."

We went next to a privately run orphanage, where seven of the " brown children " were being cared for. I saw only two. The home seemed to be a cheerful, well-managed institution and I was interested to see how happy and unselfconscious were the two small boys Peter and Dieter. And also how clean and well dressed.

Peter was rather an odd-looking child, not very dark, but with black eyes and kinky hair. Kathy told me that Peter's mother had completely rejected him when he was born, and had married a German in Giessen, keeping her connection with the Negro baby a secret. Because Giessen is a fairly large city this was possible. Peter's father she said was in America, and although he did not really think he was the father of this boy, he had signed papers accepting him as his own, and wanted to take Peter to America. In order to do this it was necessary for him to come back to Germany to get the boy, and he was willing to do this. At first permission had been given for him to return, — and then it had been withdrawn.

" Here is a father who would like to have his son," Kathy said. " Yet he cannot have him. It is hard for me to understand."

Peter's father still hoped to come. A letter one week before had said that he wanted Peter very much. But for as long a time as may be until his father can come, Peter must remain in the orphanage. If the father should lose interest, or should never be able to come at all, then Peter will be (I quote Kathy) " out of luck, poor rascal! "

The second child in the home, Dieter, whom Kathy referred to affectionately as " my heart," was a charming, lovable little boy, six years old, tall for his age, very warm and outgoing, and had a beautiful smile. Like Peter he was light, with small features and soft, shining kinky-curly hair.

" Is he not the apple of your eye? " she asked of me, when Dieter climbed up on her lap and threw his arms around her neck. " He calls me Mama, and I would like to be his mama with all my soul. And imagine — the woman who was blessed with this blessing has given permission for him to be adopted! "

Dieter's mother also was married to a German and lives in another part of Germany. She either did not know or could not remember the name of the father. Of course that father, whoever he is, has never known of the child's existence.

" Imagine when he asks about his father! " Kathy cried. " ' All children have fathers,' he will say. ' Who is *my* father? ' And when he grows up to travel maybe in the world, every Negro man of an older age he may meet, he will think, ' Maybe that man is my father! ' It makes me weep! "

The tragedy of Dieter, she said, was that he would soon be too old to be adopted because everybody wants little babies, and few children have a chance to find parents after they are six. Because of all the trouble about completing adoptions for these half-and-half children, she thought there was very little chance for Dieter ever to find a home in America.

Most of the adoptions of the half-Negro children, Kathy

said, had been in homes of Negro military couples stationed
in Germany. It is extremely difficult for couples in America to adopt them, and it rarely happens. And so a child
like Dieter, who began life in comparatively happy unselfcon-
sciousness, has little to look forward to except hard times
economically and socially in a community which hates him
because he symbolizes a triple disgrace — illegitimacy, color
difference, and defeat in war.

" To the people of Giessen," said Kathy, " these handsome,
good, and smart children born in our own city are foreigners
and enemies."

By this time it was noon, and still we had not gone to see
the Haven of Hope, nor did I know anything about Kathy
Prugel, except that she knew and loved the Negro babies. I
hesitated to ask questions, because she was conducting the
tour and our next stop was the restaurant where we had lunch.

" I want you to eat in this place, if you will," said Kathy,
" because it too is a symbol of the feeling the city of Giessen
has about the Negro children. Giessen is afraid. The
' brown baby ' reminds this city of a wicked sin. It is a
wicked sin, but it is not the sin that was done six, five, three
years ago that is important now. It is the sin that is being
done today against these children. That is important. Well,
I want you to eat in Frau Schrimpf's Brauhaus if you please."

The Brauhaus was rather plain and small, a restaurant
with a counter in the front and twenty tables without table
cloths. It was not attractive but looked clean. The most
remarkable thing was that we were the only ones there, although the hour was exactly twelve o'clock.

" You would not think that for twenty years these tables
were always full at dinner time or at lunch time and that people were standing outside waiting for places! " Kathy said.
" Until three years ago! Now, you see — nobody comes."

We sat down at a table by the window, and a waitress soon came to take our orders. After she had left us Kathy said, " Now I will tell you about Frau Schrimpf."

Frau Schrimpf was eighty years old, and had been in business in Giessen a good part of her life. At the time when the Negro soldiers were quartered there she had welcomed them into her restaurant as she welcomed everybody, without making any difference. Most of the places in Giessen had not only not welcomed Negroes, but had used every way they could, without getting into trouble with the American military, to discourage them from coming. They had given the Negroes bad food and poor service, and when possible had refused to let them in. But Frau Schrimpf had been like a grandmother to all the boys who came.

" Does not a black boy miss his home in the same way as a white one? " Kathy demanded fiercely. " Is he not lonesome and wishing for his mama? Does he not need the kindness of an old woman? "

After the " trouble " began — and by that she meant the association between Negro soldiers and German girls — the Brauhaus was banned as an eating place, and later on the Mayor himself posted a placard advising citizens of Giessen not to patronize the place which had been friendly to the " black scourge from America."

" Certainly they met the German girls at the Brauhaus," Kathy admitted. " Certainly it was a meeting place and they went from here to God knows where and what. But was it the fault of the old woman who was kind? Certainly not. It was the fault of the city officials who made no provisions for those girls, so that they were hungry and friendless. The soldiers were kind and they had money. Do you care what color he is if the money is coming and you are hungry? I guess you do not! And it was the crime of Hitler's youth organization that taught them to be prostitutes when they were children.   The German women knew that practice before any Americans came to Germany!

" So now it is empty, the Brauhaus, and soon it will close because there is no business except here and there.

" So that is why we are here," Kathy said.   " Everyone who is my guest in Giessen patronizes Frau Schrimpf's Brauhaus."

She excused herself and disappeared into the kitchen at the back.   Presently she came back with a stooped and white-haired woman who was plainly reluctant about being dragged over to my table, but tried to smile.   I stood up and shook hands with Frau Schrimpf, told her I was glad to be here, and said I had heard about her kindness to the American soldiers, and was glad of that too.   When this was interpreted to her the old lady began to cry, which was embarrassing, and hurried back to the kitchen.   Kathy followed her.

When she came back to the table where I was feeling embarrassed, conspicuous, and somewhat out of place, she told me Frau Schrimpf had said, " I thought never to see the day when I would shake hands with a white American."   We did not see her again until we were ready to leave.   But when we were on our way out, she re-appeared from the kitchen, all traces of tears carefully wiped away.   She refused to accept any money for the luncheon, which had been rather an elaborate one, and presented me with a pound of coffee.   I was touched and embarrassed again.   In Germany coffee costs five dollars a pound.

Still Kathy had not mentioned the Haven of Hope and still I had not asked her about it.   I began to feel that here was something I must be perhaps afraid of finding out about, a subject that must not be discussed.

After lunch we went to the local state orphanage for destitute children and foundlings of both colors, where there were about a dozen of the abandoned " brown babies." One was only three months old. They were beautiful children, most of them quite dark, and all more Negro in appearance than white. I thought of the kind of life any one of them had to look forward to in Giessen. Yet here and now they were in their cradles, innocent of any wrong at all.

" It is the children who will be punished," Kathy reflected. " Always when a wrong is done it is the children who are punished. I do not say that the parents were bad, but even if they were, they are not the ones who will have to pay. It is always the children and they know nothing about why they came to be born."

From the hospital we took a taxi to " Dogpatch," as Kathy called it. This was the " redlight district " (again those were her words) of the town. A good many of the white mothers, some of them married to Germans, but most unmarried, lived there with their children.

" The town is a less healthy place than this," she said. " Everybody is alike in ' Dogpatch.' "

" Dogpatch " was the same kind of little rural slum that fringes most large cities in the United States, a few rows of crude shanties, with a central pump for water, and a good deal of refuse and dirt around. There were about twenty-five houses in all, and I suppose I saw a hundred or so children.

It was a poor and shabby group that flocked around us, talking earnestly to Kathy but shying away from me. They knew her well, she said, because this was a part of her job — " Dogpatch."

Here the children, white and colored, played together without any difference between them. There were even white and colored in the same families.

Kathy said that for many of these girls prostitution began

before the war, when so many German girls were forced into
it through the youth camps, and later when they were not
provided for after they were bombed out of their homes, and
had to find places to stay wherever they could. The association with the Negro soldiers, who had money and were generous in spending it, followed almost as if it had to be.

" Mostly they weren't what you call ' good ' girls in the
first place," she said. " But nothing in Germany was provided to make them good, or to keep them good if they started
out that way.

" But there's another thing, if you will excuse me. I do
not wish to criticize America and the Americans. But this
idea about black and white we learned from your white soldiers. Listen to this. When a German woman goes to work
in a white military home, she cannot have that job if she ever
worked for Negro people when they were quartered here."

This was outdiscriminating discrimination, and I said so.

" I know it is a fact," said Kathy. " When I lost my job
being a social worker, because I helped the Negro babies
and kept them in my home, I tried to get another job. I went
and got a place as a servant, but when they found out I'd
worked for the Negro babies, well — I lost that job too."

It was the first time she had spoken about any kind of
" job." Now she went on thoughtfully, " I suppose now you
want to ask me where is this Haven of Hope. Well, you are
looking at it. I myself am the only ' haven of hope ' there is.
I had a job as a social worker until three months ago. Now
I am out of a job. You are looking at the ' color problem,'
my friend."

She laughed a little grimly at my astonishment.

" And now if you please I will show you my office. It is
the only office I have, but it is busy. I swear it is always
busy."

We climbed into a taxi and rode to Kathy's office, which of course was her own home, a two-room shack, or rather one room with a small lean-to, outside the town in a field of weeds.

" Cozy, don't you think? " she said to me. " My friends in the Red Cross found this place for me. I must not live in a room in Giessen because I cared for the ' brown babies.' So this is home for me and my own two children."

Sitting in the one comfortable chair in Kathy's living room-bedroom-office I heard her story, a tragic and fantastic one, colored by her vivid, colloquial, careless English. Kathy herself is one of the many displaced persons in Germany. Her story seemed to me especially significant because she had made her own adjustment through service to another group that was an unfortunate by-product of World War II.

CHAPTER TWENTY-TWO

The Story of Kathy

The story of Kathy (as she told it to me) began with a handsome house in East Prussia, where there was room and light and comfort and plenty of food, a handsome husband who liked to go out socially, and two small daughters, as lovely as two flowers. Her husband was in the army, although he was not a storm trooper. During his absences from home, Kathy herself took part in the underground opposition to the Nazis. The big handsome house became a station for people fleeing from the Nazis.

"Why did I do it?" she asked. "I cannot say. Perhaps because I had a heart and a mind. In war people lose both. And — well, they would come to the house, and I would keep them there until the priest in the town (and he was a saint) would get them taken out of Germany. Some went in boats by the North Sea. Some went to France. There was a group of people in the town working like that.

"We had to pretend the refugees were servants, and make excuses when the house was searched by the storm troopers. It was dangerous. But it filled your heart. I am one for danger!" she exclaimed.

"Now there is not the same kind of danger, but my mind seems to keep ready for the knock on the door and ready to think right away what to say to a policeman. I am trained by all this to be an actress, to make up a story." She added hastily, "But I am not a liar, I swear. What I tell you now is the truth. That is another thing we learned. It was how to look at the person who claimed to be one of us. We learned to know by looking at that one whether we could trust him, and to know how much to tell him. We learned. But some of us died before we learned."

One of the refugees was a young French girl who had been captured in Paris and carried to Germany as a prisoner. Through the priest in the town, who led the underground and visited the prisoners, she escaped and was brought to Kathy's house where she stayed secretly for seventeen months before she was discovered. Both the girl and Kathy were tried and sentenced to be imprisoned at Buchenwald.

" That would be the end for us," she said. " I did not mind for myself so much but I was sorry for the French girl. And I was frightened for my two babies. My husband was gone, and I must not get him in the trouble. But," she continued somewhat bitterly, " it did not matter. When they sent for him he would no longer claim me as his wife. It was necessary to save himself. I would not be able to save myself that way."

" The German officer in the town was a storm trooper, but he had a heart like human people, as my husband did not have. He liked my babies and managed to postpone my imprisonment for a month, and in that month, almost as if it were a miracle planned by God especially for me and the girls, the Americans invaded Europe and entered the town where I lived.

" So there we were, and the people said, ' It is the American devils! They will kill us all! This is the end for us! ' so I thought: What is there to lose? I went to the American headquarters alone and talked English to the captain in command! " She smiled grimly. " That is another thing I learned — to do the things I could not do. But it was easy in the end and I did not care. I had made a bargain with God and said I would ask for nothing, not my life even, if he would let my children be safe and healthy."

Kathy then shifted ahead in her story as if she must prove that her prayer had been answered. " It may seem strange to you, but that is just what He did. We lost everything in the world. The Americans took my house. We have not anything today except food to eat, and sometimes we have no food. But my girls have never been hurt by anybody and they are healthy. I believe in God! "

Then she went back to her story.

" Well, I spoke the best English I could, and it was not very good then, and I told the American captain what had happened in my house. I told him, ' This French girl has been in my house for seventeen months in secret. I have two children, ten and seven. They are girls. I ask you to take this French girl to Paris where she lives and give her to her family. And I ask you to take care of my little children. That is all. If there is any punishment for me because I am German and your enemy, well, I will take it.'

" So the Americans were not devils after all. The French girl went back to Paris, and I heard that she came to her people and I was glad. And my children were safe. And I — " she giggled. " The devils gave me a job as a social worker! They were good devils. We were happy, I tell you.

" But then they made the Russian zone and the American and French zones. That I could not bear. But it was the American soldiers that helped me to go to Kassel with my little girls. I think there was a rule they broke, but we went. And that was the beginning of life for me! "

Kathy stopped again, stood up and walked over to the window. Several minutes passed and I sat there quietly. It was so still that I could hear the ticking of the clock across the room on a shelf. She came away from the window and sat down again on the bed.

"Yes, that was when my life began," she said, as if she had never stopped at all. "It was the first time I faced and looked straight at — what shall I say — good and bad, and decided myself what was good and bad, and it didn't matter what was said by other people. I was not a young woman even then. I had two little girls, and they would have to suffer because I decided something was right. I knew all that. But there in Kassel — well, I was born there."

There were, among the American troops in Kassel, some Negroes. This was the place where Kathy first met the "brown-baby" problem and this was what led her to her unusual dedication.

While working there in Kassel as a social worker, one day she passed a schoolyard where children were playing. On the outside, leaning against a high fence that enclosed the playing space, she saw the "blondy" (Kathy's word for the young woman).

"I thought at first this is a school child. She was crying, and I said to her, 'Sweetie, why are you not in there playing with the others?' Then I saw. She was a child. I was right about that. But she was pregnant and she was sick and she was afraid.

"It was a time you do not ask any other questions. You do something. I took her to the room where I stayed with my daughters. And after she felt better she told me. The father of the child was an American, not married to her. And he was a Negro. This girl lived in a family with eight people, but she had gone away from them. She was afraid to tell her father. She stayed alone. And the Negro man was gone.

"I did not ask any more questions either. I knew the answer. Plenty girls were hungry then. If there are eight in your family you will be hungry. Plenty girls had babies. I made that girl go to bed, and told her we'd do something tomorrow.

" Well, I sat in the chair all night and I never went to bed myself. I asked myself questions. I was brought up in a strict home. Good girls married. Bad girls had babies but they didn't marry. Well, I read the Bible. I read about Jesus and the bad woman.

" Then I asked, ' What does black and white mean? ' I never saw any black people except the Americans. And I swear they were not as proud as some white ones I knew. They were good. Except the color, I could not find any difference.

" Then I asked, ' What about this little baby that is not born yet? Will it not be helpless like my own babies? Will it not cry and laugh and be hungry like my own? ' I have asked God to keep my children safe and healthy. Do I not help another woman's child because that woman is not married? Or because the child is black?

" I knew as if somebody said it. That was my job, the black child. That was what I had to do.

" I asked, ' What will become of my own children? ' I do not care what happens to me, but I care what happens to them. I do not care what people think of me. But I care what those children think and I care what people think of my children.

" Well, I thought God would take care of them. They are people like me. They will have their chance. I will work twice as hard. I will help the black child to have a chance too.

" It seemed as if God said, ' If you help my black children, I help your white ones! ' It seemed as if God made a bargain with me that time! "

The next morning Kathy went herself to that family of eight, to pave the way for the girl to come home and have her baby. Perhaps they were not hard to persuade. Perhaps, even, she described her night of decision to them. But whatever way she used, the family accepted the daughter and the baby. The local priest refused to baptize the baby, but Kathy secured the Negro army chaplain in a nearby town, and she stood as godmother to the baby, which was " brown as a walnut," she said, and was named Katherine.

For this piece of service she had her first taste of what her decision would require of her. She almost lost her job, and she lost some of her friends. But perhaps through the help of the military she kept working until another incident happened which forced her to leave Kassel.

Late one evening she came upon two girls standing on the bridge over the river. She said her work took her walking at all hours of the night. One of the girls was carrying a baby on a pillow, and she was weeping. When Kathy asked the trouble they tried not to answer, but finally the second girl confessed that the baby of her sister was a Negro, and since there was no food to be had for a " brown baby " in Kassel, they had decided it would be better to drown it in the river, rather than see it starve to death before their eyes.

" So I said, ' You are a good girl. You cannot drown a human life in the river! Come with me! ' "

So Kathy took the girl with her baby to her room, as she had taken the first girl with the unborn child. She kept them for a week and later found a place where they could stay.

But for herself, she was warned to leave Kassel. Her services as a social worker were no longer wanted. And her employers considered her a bad member of society, having disobeyed one warning.

From Kassel, Kathy and her two little girls, both now of

school age, went to Giessen and there she found a job with the Red Cross.

By this time the " brown-baby " situation in Giessen had become a bitter one because of the large number of American Negro troops quartered there. White girls with " brown babies " did not dare to appear on the street because they and the babies were likely to be stoned. Kathy herself was stoned at one time when she carried a " brown baby " in her arms through the streets.

In 1949 Kathy began working on her plan for her Haven of Hope, which was to be a home where such children could live and be cared for. She was a convincing talker, and managed to interest a good many private individuals who were sympathetic, and she found a good deal of interest among the Negro soldiers. But the newspapers heard of the new project and a furor was aroused. Only one paper supported it. At Radio Frankfurt the operators read the one favorable article and were inspired to invite her to come and make a speech over the radio about the Haven of Hope.

She prepared a good speech, she thought, and practiced it and made over an old dress to wear in Frankfurt. But on the morning the broadcast was to take place, there was a letter from the station saying it had been canceled. No reason was given. The next day a brief article appeared in an English-language newspaper, advising readers that the American military group had not sanctioned the project, and that the authorities opposed it. Kathy showed me the article.

" That was the way they told my friends, the Negro soldiers, that they must not give me money! " she said bitterly. " I think it was their way of saying that America was not to blame for the ' brown-baby ' problem. Anyway there would be no nice building and home for our children." She stopped and then said slowly, " But there is still the Haven of Hope! "

The hardest part of this whole thing was the effect the publicity had on her own daughters.

" They came from school every day scratched and beaten," she said. " Other children followed them all the way to their house, and they said their mother was a ' nigger lover.' I sent the older one to a boarding school because she had been persecuted most, but she came back. ' You cannot get the money, Mama,' she said first. But I said I would get the money. Then she said, ' Not even if you get the money, Mama, I want to stay. This is my job, too.' I was happy, I tell you. But I was afraid. I *am* afraid! "

It was at that time that the Giessen officials asked Kathy to move out of the city, and Red Cross friends found the house in the field of weeds for her and her daughters.

" I wondered why they did not fire me from my job also," she said. " I think maybe it was because somebody had to take care of the half-and-halfs, and they were glad to have somebody who wanted to care for them."

Sometime before this the Unitarian Service Committee in America had heard about the first ideas for a Haven of Hope. " That is the way God does, I guess," she said. " One thing goes. Another thing comes. Boxes and bundles of clothing and toys began coming soon after I had moved to the shanty. All of them were addressed to Haven of Hope and sent in my care.

" I kept the boxes and used them for the children. In the town they accused me of ' getting rich off the Americans,' but I swear it all went to the children. I was the Haven of Hope even without a building. There was no other Haven of Hope for the ' brown babies.' "

To centers in Munich and Frankfurt as well as Giessen she took clothing which was distributed through large " parties " arranged in churches or homes, for the mothers with their babies, the white as well as the brown.

" We never made a difference between them," she explained. " The troubles of the brown children are worse, but there is no difference between poor and hungry children.

" I want to tell you about the parties," she said, " because they are the beginning of hope for the brown babies. To these parties they come, the white and the brown children, and their mothers. Here they are treated the same. Here they eat and play together and are happy. Here the white may learn to know the brown, the brown may trust the white. And here those other people who help, and the visitors who come — sometimes even the police who come because of suspicion — may have a lesson seeing all of these together.

" I like to think of these people, even sometimes of the police! Most people are kind if they are not afraid, I think. Here at the parties they are not afraid. Nobody is afraid! These people have read in the newspaper and heard the stories about that ' black scourge.' But when they see these children playing they will say, ' Is this then the black scourge? But it is only little children! They could not be bad, so young, so sweet they are! ' And they must love them — the brown as the white — because the child is always the door to the heart!

" Is it not like the Bible — that a little child will lead the way? I think that here in Germany we might find out how to make a lesson for the Americans! "

But it only sounded easy and simple as she told it. For the parties themselves were hard for Kathy, as the word went out to people and officials who had not been present to see the sweet and innocent children with their own eyes. They could not believe the reports. They talked about the " black scourge." In Frankfurt and Kassel and Munich things were not so bad, but it was very hard in Giessen, where, she felt, the problem was bigger and more complex. After every one of those parties Kathy had trouble with the police. She was even accused of using the choice boxes for brown babies and denying the white ones their share. Her house was searched and robbed time after time. All mail which she sent out with her name was likely to be censored and confiscated.

" Did you see that I wrote you the postal card, and that I signed it ' Kathy '? " she asked. " It was only partly to be friendly. I want to be friendly of course. But it was more to be sure you would get it that I did not use my name. It might have reached you. But it might not. I do not always know."

This uncertainty about getting mail through, she told me, is one of the reasons that the Unitarians in America know so little about the Haven of Hope, and have never known that it is not a thriving settlement house.

" I am going to tell them," she said. " But I am not permitted to tell the whole truth. As long as the boxes continue to come I will use them as the senders wish. I do not mean to deceive anybody but I wish to do the job for the children."

I asked her if what she had told me was for quotation if I wished to quote it, and she gave me her permission — but not too eagerly.

" If you tell it, will you tell it just as I have told you? " she asked earnestly. " Do not add one word, either good or bad, or take away one word from what I said, if you please."

After the most recent party, which had been held in a church in Giessen just about three months before, she received word that she would have no further salary as a social worker. She might work if she wished but there would be no money. American Red Cross workers who sympathized with her gave her gifts, all of which she had sold so that she might continue to work for the children.

This was the time when she took the quickly-ended job as servant with an American military couple. After that she had not tried again to get a paying position, for her " job without pay " took most of her time. Her older daughter, she said, had learned to write on a typewriter. It would help a little.

" Perhaps the way of fortune will change very soon," she said. " I cannot complain, for the bargain I made has been kept on both sides. I asked only that my children be safe and healthy. In return I said I would work. And it has happened just that way.

" But always there is something that helps along for the next day. My work is for the half-and-halfs. When the boxes come I will divide the things. When I have made a child happy it also fills my stomach as well as my heart. I am the happiest woman I know."

That seemed to be the end of the story, but while we sat there in the shack, which now looked more like a palace to me, and while I thought it over, she suddenly exclaimed, " But I have forgotten the interesting part! I did not tell you of the nights when the bombs came, and when I wrapped the children in blankets and we stayed in the hills. Sometimes I did not leave the hills for three or four days except to run down and look for food. I have forgotten to tell you the most exciting part of my story! "

CHAPTER TWENTY-THREE

My Dear Tatjana

The day I arrived in Diepholz, Germany, to be the guest of the Lithuanian School of February Sixteenth, I went to bed with mumps. If there can be any less dignified interlude in the experience of a research traveler I don't know it. On the other hand the situation provided me with an unexpected opportunity.

In searching for a way to tell about the Lithuanian refugees — the small violinist who serenaded outside my window each evening, the little girls who brought wild flowers, the principal who sent a message thanking me for being sick because it gave his school a chance to " help an American," and Tatjana Klopfmüller who was my nurse, my book of information and my good friend — in thinking of all these people I have decided to share a letter I have written to Tatjana.

My dear Tatjana:

This letter is to tell you that I have not forgotten and will never forget the Lithuanian School of February Sixteenth. I shall remember the kindness of your children and staff, and your own devoted labors as " physician," during what must have been a trying and interminable week for you. But mostly I shall remember you and your people because of the warmth and patience and gaiety of your spirit.

The School of February Sixteenth! There surely was never another school with such a name. You told me it was for the day of Lithuania's independence, February 16th, 1918, when you declared yourselves " an independent democratic state."

I shall never forget the first shivery day when I came.

You may remember that the Lithuanian district supervisor brought me from Bremen in his little English automobile with the steering wheel on the right-hand side. Mr. Zunde met me at the Bremen Neighborhood House, a modern settlement efficiently directed, and supported by the Unitarian Service Committee. When we started out, one of the first things Mr. Zunde said was that we'd see quite a different kind of place at Diepholz.

" We are poor! " he said simply and eloquently. Then he told me about your school.

He said (and you never mentioned this to me, Tatjana, nor did anyone else there) that your school was for " hard-core " refugees, and was taught by a " hard-core " staff. I was prepared, then, to find a place that would look a little like a hospital or a sanatorium, as well as a school.

He said it was located in a D.P. camp, in a low and damp section of Germany, and therefore cheap, and I knew that the school itself was housed in an old German army barracks.

But no one could be prepared for anything so dreary as that school building. You've grown accustomed to it, and you see it as a haven for children. I learned to see it so too, but the first look was a shock. Perhaps there is something about a former barracks that is more dreary than other places. The tall blank building and the rows and rows of windows were in themselves forbidding. But added to this were the ugly scars made by bombs and shrapnel. What repairs had been made were badly done, with no effort to match up parts.

" This," I thought, " is not a good place even for the army. But for children — and sick children — impossible! "

Well, we drove into a big open court, stopped in front of the building, and climbed up the broken steps leading to the half-open front door. I did not notice until later that it was off the hinge at the top. Everything about that building was a shambles.   The hallway was dark and dreary, and vast and cold.

The big dining room where we were taken at once for lunch looked more like an assembly hall, with a small stage at one end, and rows of benches.   There were long tables too, pushed back against the walls.   The food was boiled potatoes, black bread and *ersatz* coffee.   This was my introduction to coffee made of roasted cereals, and believe it or not I liked the *ersatz*, maybe because it was hot, and the place and the day and I were all so terribly cold.   The dishes were chipped enamelware.   But the food and the dishes and the table were clean.   It continued to amaze me, throughout the week, that in all this crowded, awkward, threadbare kind of life there could still be cleanliness.

On that day the room was empty of children except for two or three little big-eyed girls who carried dishes from the table to the kitchen for washing, and stared at me sideways while they made their trips back and forth.   But I knew that some-where in that building there were two hundred boys and girls.

The staff members did not become individuals to me then. None of them could speak English and all of us clung close to Mr. Zunde, who was the only one to help us understand each other.   When he said good-bye, and it appeared we were about to be left alone with each other in the dining room, I think we were all a little terrified.   It is frightening not to be able to exchange one single question or answer.

Then came a flash of sunshine across the gloom and here were you from somewhere, five feet high with four-inch heels (you do make use of the spikeheels that come in the bundles from America!), your eyes as bright and blue as two African violets, and your hair hanging in gold curls to your shoulders.

I thought you must be one of the students.   When they all sighed with relief, and Mr. Zunde introduced you as " the teacher of English " I was surprised. When later I learned that you speak five languages, among them those impossible ones, Hungarian and Russian, I was amazed.

I remember your first hesitating English words, " You-are-welcome! " They were no less warm (although we were strangers) than your farewell a week later: " Thank you for coming. Thank you for being sick, so that we might become friends! "

" You-are-welcome! " you said, and I began to think I might live after all, for here was a fairy princess who could understand me when I would eventually have to confess that I was feeling ghastly. You said that you had never spoken to an American before. " I speak English uneasily," you said, but I understood you easily. I was so very glad to meet you, Tatjana.

You asked if I'd like to take a walk around the refugee camp before going to my room, and it seemed a good idea, because if that walk didn't take place at once I knew it never would. You grasped my arm, assuming your responsibility as hostess to the American visitor, and propelled me firmly out through the swinging door, down the steps and across the D.P. wasteland.

The excursion was rather fruitless, as an excursion, for I couldn't see clearly enough even to be disturbed at that moment by the ruins, the half-collapsed buildings where families were living, the great hole in the earth where a bomb had made a direct hit, the shattered little chapel where you held your " church." It was too cold, and I was too nearly dead.

When at last the excursion was ended, you walked me back to the barracks and showed me the room where I would be staying, with my bags already placed in it.

That room was a tall square box with the plaster gray and cracking. For furniture it had a narrow army cot and a table and a basin with a single forlorn water tap, dripping and turning green to boot. But how proud you were of the " running water " in the guestroom! It was next to your own, which had not the luxury of running water. I learned days later that to save me from being bothered you had been running up and down a flight of stairs and the length of two long drafty halls, carrying pitchers of water for your own use and mine.

We stood there for a moment, and then I must have begun to turn green like the water faucet, for you looked stricken, and you cried, " Forgive us! The guestroom is not good enough. You must go to the hotel in the village. You are sick! "

But Tatjana, I swear it was the sickness and not the room which made me turn green. For how you'd prepared the guestroom! There on the table were the two neat stacks of books about Lithuania (all in English), with the picture ones on top, and for lighter moments six old copies of the *Reader's Digest*. There was a fresh new scratch pad with two long needle-sharp pencils laid straight side by side. To be sure this was meant to be the room of a writer, you said, and a writer would need pencils. And there was the great bouquet of blue field daisies on the table.

I think you began to like me and to like Americans when I declared that the room was beautiful, that a hotel in Diepholz would not be half so nice, and I wasn't sick but a little tired and would be all right tomorrow. Your anxious blue eyes searching mine intently and with concern grew softer and you smiled. Then as if with one job done you were more than ready for the next, you clapped your hands and said firmly:

" Thank you! Thank you from my heart. And now you *are* sick. I shall be the physician. I shall dispense the medicines. I shall tell you what to do and you will do it. I tell you to go to bed."

Into that hard cot with a sinking place in the center where the springs broke apart, I tumbled obediently. Underneath the feather bed where, for the first time in many days, it felt warm, I stayed for a week, because of course you were right as always. When the doctor came the next morning he said it was mumps. And that was that.

Well, you laughed until you cried and said it was a great joke, and very kind and thoughtful of me at the same time to have anything so absurd. Joke or not, for a week I lay there, staring at that dreary ceiling, hating myself for being sick, hating to have you wait on me, as you did intrepidly, hating the way I looked, and the way the doctor looked, and choking on the oranges and eggs and real coffee you brought me in quantities. Oranges were twenty-five cents apiece and coffee five dollars a pound, and well I knew that you and your people had not tasted either one for years, and had not had your salaries of something like ten dollars a month paid to you for nearly half a year. Once you said to me, " Why are you displeased at making it possible for us to give? It has been so long since there was anyone we could give to."

You chattered in English while you darted about waiting on me. I was charmed with the way you twittered and flitted, birdlike, making that bare room light with your cheerfulness.

Outside the window all evening the children sang their sweet, sad folksongs, with one of the boys playing his accordion, and another the violin, sweetly and plaintively. On the first evening when the serenade awakened me from a nap, I thought I was dreaming, but you explained that the music was for me. After that I looked forward to the serenade just after supper every night.

" Who can play the violin so well? " I asked one time.

" You shall see the little violinist. You shall see my Pranas! " you declared, and promptly drew back the shutters from the window overlooking the court where the boys and girls had gathered. They looked up when the shutters opened and the singing faltered but went on again. Some of them waved. Standing on one side was the violinist, a little boy, four feet high perhaps, with a small fiddle tucked under his chin, one hand on the strings while the other sawed away earnestly. His eyes were on those strings, and he did not look up until the tune was finished. Then shyly Pranas raised his eyes from the fiddle. They were black as midnight. Even from so far away I could see the long curling lashes. Then he looked down again in confusion and you closed the shutters.

" It is too cold," you said. Outside the violin went on playing " Träumerei," and " Santa Lucia " and " My Old Kentucky Home," a rambling incongruous repertoire strangely in keeping with the room, the forlorn dripping water faucet and the cracked walls, and an American patient with mumps, in a Lithuanian school in a German D.P. camp.

" Tell me about the little violinist," I said to you.

You told me then your first story.

" He is nine and he is very beautiful, as you say. He is the son of a musician, a very great musician, but the man his father is — dead."

Something about the hesitation in your voice made me ask, " How did his father die? " You told me that the man had died when the family, the father, the mother and the little boy fled from Lithuania together in 1944.

" It was so cold," you explained. " There was no shelter. There was so little food. It was in the throat and the lung, the sickness. But the baby was well. The boy today is healthy! " (You said it gaily as if you were saying it rained yesterday but it is bright today.) " The boy is healthy and he carries his father in him. It is a good thing."

" He carries his father in him," I repeated after you, thinking of the music, and you nodded with that same bright smile.

" Yes, he is a Lithuanian," you said.

" He carries Lithuania in him," I interpreted, and you nodded again.

" Thank you! That is what I mean! "

" Do you think he is really a talented violinist, the little boy? " I asked.

" He will be a very great musician if he lives to be old and if he can study," you answered. " I hope that he may study."

" Tell me about Lithuania," I said then. " I don't know a thing about Lithuania."

Then you told me about your country.

" Lithuania, my country! " You said the words as if they made a song you loved to sing. " It is not a very big country, but it is good. There are not many big cities either, but many farms, and we had much milk and butter there and fruits growing. And the big city, that was Vilnius. I think it might be a little like New York, but not so big nor so fine certainly as the American city. Vilnius " — again the word was a song — " Vilnius was the capital city first, and after the Poles came and took it, then we moved to Kaunas. All this I can remember very well."

You told me of the great age of your country and your people, how they had been powerful in ancient times, and how the Latin historian in his books had written about these powerful people.

" We are descendants of a great race of people," you said with pride. " And we are a kind people. I believe we are — what is your English word — civilized. We have been kind even to our enemies although Lithuania was not always a Christian country."

You told me about your religion. One time you called my attention to an unusually beautiful flower, a purple flower, which one of the children had brought for a vase on the table.

" It is beautiful! " you said. " If God does not live in this beautiful flower then he does not live."

But now, explaining that ancient belief and the modern one, you said, " I would like to talk about our religion because it is the reason that our people are as they are. We are simple. We are close to what grows. We are close to God. We are so simple that we believe God is life. If God is in us, the Lithuanians, then he is in others also. It would be against our religion to turn against other people. That would be turning against God."

" What about the people who turned against you? " I asked. " Was that God turning against you? "

You looked distressed.

" I do not understand! " you confessed. " Perhaps there is something else, the devil. We do not always know which is God and which is the devil. But we believe that God is there and here. That is all I can tell you." You looked about to cry. " We are such very simple people. Forgive me! " You thought a moment.

" But it is something like this. Someone said, ' The Americans are machines for making money.' But I said, ' The Americans are fathers and mothers and children also.' So I was glad when you were sick because if Americans were machines they would not have the mumps! "

So that was why you were all so pleased about my illness! Being neither a father nor a mother nor exactly a child, I was glad, even to be horrid-looking with that great greasy bandage around my jaws, to prove to you I was certainly not a machine.

You told me about the new Lithuanian state, about that independence day of 1918 when the flags waved, and you were a government all your own, recognized even by my own " great country," as you were careful to call it. You told me

how your people worked and studied and tried to show yourselves approved for statehood. You told me how you and
your father and mother lived and prospered at Vilnius, the
capital city, and how you went to school and learned to speak
so many languages.

" It is good to know another tongue," you said. " It is
the window to another people."

You told me about your father, who died in the war with
Poland, when Poland took half your new nation, and you and
your mother fled from Vilnius to Kaunas and became refugees.

You told how small Lithuania struggled to be neutral in
the conflict between Germany and Russia, how Germany occupied your country for a time, and how finally in this tug of
war between the two big enemies Lithuania's few cities and
many farms fell to the Soviets. You told how thousands were
deported to Siberia, other thousands were enslaved in Lithuania, and how you and your widowed mother escaped to
Germany, refugees again with thousands more like you.

You found a place to work as a stenographer in Leipzig
because of your skill with languages, and you left your
mother at Dresden. Then came the bombing of Dresden by
the Americans, and you told how you had searched the ruined
city seeking your mother. It was three days, you said, before
you found her, and all around you as you searched were the
dead and the wounded. You told me then how you had come
at last to Diepholz, to be a teacher.

" This school is a refuge for many, as well as for the children," you declared. " We are so poor, and yet we have
much. We have safety, and the roof. We have traveled so
long! "

" You must hate the big countries," I said finally. " You
must hate Germany and Russia — and America too — with
a terrible hate."

You looked a little astonished. " We have no room in our minds for hate," you said. " We have much to think about. Each day is a new problem to solve. We have our children. We must keep them healthy. One must have *time* to hate. It is for people with time."

I tried to argue with you, to say that it doesn't take any time to hate, that you can do it on the side, or like listening to the radio while you're doing other things. That only bewildered you. You said you had no radio to listen to. Then I said at least it could give you some personal satisfaction to indulge in a good healthy hatred. You were puzzled again.

" Satisfaction? " you asked. " Healthy hatred? I do not know what you mean. Forgive me, my English is so very poor."

After a moment you said suddenly, " Let me tell you another story."

" This is about a good Russian, no doubt," I said.

" Yes, you are right. How did you know? " you asked. " Americans are so smart! "

Then you told the story.

" It was when we lived at Kaunas, after the Poles took Vilnius away. The Russians came, and then Mama and I were living in two rooms. Mama's room had the window. She was even then a little blind and she liked to sit by the window.

" The Russian soldier came to our door and we were frightened. But he was kind. He said to Mama, ' Mother, my wife is sick, and we have no room. Will you give us a room, please? ' Mama gave them the room with the window because there were two and would soon be three. And Mama slept with me in the room at the back. The soldier was very kind. He came to us with meat and flour. There was no one then who had meat, and we were lucky. When the baby came it was a little girl and it had my Mama's name. And how she loved that little one — as if it were her own child! "

" What happened to the Russian? " I asked.

" That was a good thing," you said. " When Mama and I must go to Germany the Russian soldier helped us to get away. He hired the cart himself and made the plan for Mama and me to cross the border into Germany. We had a message one time from the woman. The soldier was killed later. Mama grieved so sadly."

" Are you never homesick to go back to Lithuania? " I asked her. " Do you never grieve for what you have lost? "

You hesitated.

" I am lonely for my country," you admitted, " and for my friends I grieve. But it is better not to grieve. We are alive. I have a room, one room for me. So many have not rooms to live in. I have all of the children. I have much."

" Do you think it is right for any big nation to swallow up a little one? " I persisted. " Do you think it should be allowed to happen? "

Again you hesitated, but it was not the English words which troubled you. At last you said, " Forgive me for being slow. I am not able to say what is right or wrong. For many years I have not known any except people who have lost everything. I cannot quite remember how it is to own things — a house, a garden. I grieve sometimes because I must always receive and be the beggar. And I grieve because I cannot be the one to give. That may be a sin. But what I am trying to say is perhaps we will all find that we were wrong to possess those things in the beginning."

I was reproved. I was afraid.

" But then," and you laughed, " when one has nothing, there is nothing to lose. Is it not so? "

CHAPTER TWENTY-FOUR

When Giedra Speaks Again

The first day when you, Tatjana, my " physician," said it was safe for the children to come near a patient recovering from the mumps, they came to call in twos and threes, mostly the little ones for they were most curious to look at an American. The glimpse they'd had from the window had not been reassuring.

Except for their speech, they might have been American children. There were blonde ones and dark ones, some looking like Scandinavians, some almost like Arabs. The small violinist might have been a child from Casa Materna in Naples. They were thin, which was my only reminder that most of these youngsters had family histories of tuberculosis and were either in mild stages of the disease themselves, or were predisposed to it. The subject was never discussed except when I questioned you directly. Once you said, " We are thankful for this place. It does not look fine to you, but it is beautiful to us, because for so many of our children it is life instead of death."

Some were orphans, but many had parents living in this very D.P. camp and other camps in Germany. The younger ones were more likely to be healthy, you told me, because in the flight from their homes the babies were the ones to be protected, fed when there was no food, sheltered when there was no shelter for the older ones.

" The fathers and mothers wrapped the only coat around

the smallest one to keep him from freezing. The others could move about and walk and run and keep shaking themselves to be warm.

" I think it must be so in all the world where people live. It is the little ones to be saved, and that is right. They are helpless. They make us unselfish. But with our own people there was another reason. Let the older die, if someone dies, but the small ones must grow to be Lithuania someday."

I asked if you really thought they would go back there sometime, and if you thought there would again be a Lithuanian state.

" I believe it can be, if it is to be," you said. " And perhaps it might be soon. These things happen quickly. In history it has happened that way. Another war might give us a state. Some want another war for that reason, I am sorry. I do not want war. There is something, not statehood, that I wish these little ones to live for. Perhaps they will stay here always in Germany. Perhaps some will go to another country, to America. I would like them to be better Americans because they carry Lithuania to America also."

The children began to come in pairs and small groups. The first knocks were timid and soft, but later they grew louder after the first brave ones had told the not-so-brave ones what had happened in the sickroom.

Regina and Giedra brought bouquets of wild flowers, stubby bunches with short stems, picked by their very own hands. At first those two stood in the doorway staring at me and clutching their bouquets, too shy to come closer. You said pleasant things to them in Lithuanian which must have been reassuring, for they moved slowly forward, close together, and then courtseyed.

Regina, you told me, had been born after her parents escaped from their homeland. Both were sick in the D.P.

camp. " This one " — and you curled one of the pale, straw-colored locks around your finger — " this Regina is like a song from a farm in Lithuania. Is she not beautiful? " She was, with a transparent white skin, clean-cut features and mild blue eyes.

But it was the other, the dark-eyed one, that I looked at most. Her name was Giedra. Her hair was cut short, and it was not combed very neatly. She looked angry somehow, and tragic and stubborn. While Regina at your suggestion handed her bunch of flowers to me timidly, Giedra threw hers onto the bed, and looked the other way toward the door. When you spoke to her she did not answer or look at you, and you put your arm about her then, and said to me with a voice full of compassion, " Forgive us. She cannot help it."

Giedra must have understood, for she pulled at Regina's hand and the two hurried away.

" I must tell you about our dear child Giedra," you said to me. " She is rude but she does not intend to be unkind. She is a sick child."

" Giedra — tubercular? " I said in surprise.

" No, certainly not. Her body is well, but she has memories which waken her in the night."

Your eyes filled with tears in that quick way they had.

" I do not know what is the greatest of all sins, but I think it must be the wrong that is done to a little child," you said. " We have spoken about hating. Only that one thing I believe one must hate.

" You saw the sad eyes of Giedra. This child lived, with her father and her mother and her brother at Klaepeda. That is a harbor on the Baltic Sea. They fled in 1943. Giedra was a baby only three years old. They left their house without taking anything, only the clothes they wore, and they walked from the city, hiding in sheds on the way, until they came to a wood. When they reached the road, they must ride a bus because they could not walk any farther. But there were four of them and they might be seen. It would be better not to go all together.

" The father would take the little girl and get on the first bus. The mother would take the little boy and go into the woods. Giedra waited with her father at this place. She heard a noise and her father fell dead from the bullet. The little girl did not understand, but the father would not speak. Giedra ran back into the woods the way her mother had gone with the brother. She called and cried and the mother came, but they could not go back to the road. Those three, with the father dead, went on through the woods until they came to a village. People helped them there. So they made their way to Germany. But it was too hard for the mother. Her mind went away, and the little girl stayed with other people. The boy went away to find work, and she has never seen him. Giedra has remembered all these things. For nine years she has remembered."

You stopped. " Well, that is all. We fight a battle here against the memories. We love her very much, this sad child, and we shall perhaps win over the memories. She is much better. But you see, she *cannot speak*. She has not spoken for nine years."

You said that in all the years there had been no one able to be close to her until at last she found little Regina. Although Giedra never spoke even to her, they must be always together.

" The little Regina did not look smart to you," you said. " And she is not smart, but she is of good will. She is the first to be loved by Giedra. When a child can love, then a great thing has happened."

You told me how Giedra had come to the school.

" The poor dark-eyed silent one! The family that kept her brought her here. ' We tried to help her! ' they said. ' We were kind to her. But she is stubborn. She does not hear, or does not wish to hear. She walks alone.' And they said, ' Is she sick then, or only dumb? ' But our principal is a very wise man and he knew, because it has happened before that the muscles of the throat were locked because the muscles of the mind and heart were locked.

" Often I have sat with this child, and while she was silent and dumb I was myself for her. In me there was what she must feel. And first I wanted to cry out, but I must not because to speak would be to know the Thing is so. When no word escapes perhaps it is not so!

" And I would think then that I was Giedra. Inside my heart there would try to be the evil that only my eyes had seen when I was three and my mind could not understand. But then I am an older Giedra, and I hear the things that other people say, and must begin to know what happened when I was four. I want to cry out again against it. But something stops, because my good, small, innocent heart has no thought to express a thing so vile, so bad. And I am dumb.

" And then I am Giedra, afraid of the time when I might say the thoughts. When I shall speak they will be true. Then I am myself of the evil."

" But do you really believe this child can think these things?" I asked you.

" Certainly not! " you said. " Something in her, not the mind, may think them. It locks the muscles of the speech. It hides from her what she must not remember.

" Forgive me. All these things I have thought because I love this Giedra so deeply. She carries a heavy burden. But it grows lighter. You see, she has found a friend. She trusts the little Regina, who is not very smart. But she is pure, she is beautiful, she is without guile. And our doctor says the operation can come soon. When Giedra is ready she will go to the hospital."

" When will that be, do you think? " I asked.

" Who knows? But it will happen. Giedra will speak."

" I wonder what she will say," I said curiously.

You were silent for a long time and finally you spoke slowly.

" It is something I am afraid to think. I have asked the doctor about other children. Some say foolish things. Our Giedra is not foolish or simple. She is deep inside. For nine years she has been alone there. Perhaps it is fear she will express. Perhaps it may be hate. Perhaps — it may be for the little Regina.

" I do not know. I dare not try to know. But I think the whole world must be still and listen to what shall come out of those years of silence — when Giedra speaks again."

" Will you let me know? " I asked you eagerly. " Will you write and tell me what she says? "

You said you wrote English uneasily, but you promised to let me know.

At last the great day came for walking around once more, and seeing all that I had come so far to see. Concerned even then for my health, you led me about swathed in a heavy wool scarf, the one you provided, and washed before you gave it to me, so that I would feel as if it were more truly my own.

I visited the classrooms in that dreary barracks building that did not seem so much like a barracks now, nor so dreary. Some of the rooms were big and barnlike, some were more like cells; only a few had desks. All at least had benches.

The rooms were cold. But they had always been cold, without heat all through the winter. The children who had coats wore them to class, you told me, in winter.

I had my first meal in the dining room with all the boys and girls, still with that wool scarf tied around my throat (and how courteously they all pretended to ignore it). There were the same potatoes, and black bread, but now it was pleasant bread.

I was almost ready for bed again, but you told me to wait while the chairs were pushed back because there was something else to come. The folk dancers had prepared a program for me and you prayed me to be so kind as to wait and see what the children had prepared. I came quickly to life again with the first wild weird note of the accordion and thrilled, weak as I was, to the color of the costumes — the girls in their bright embroidered skirts, and the boys in their gay green sashes.

Here was Lithuania, here was your country, living and strong and gay, as it was meant to be. The spirit of the dances was contagious, exhilarating. The figures were violent, gay, intricate. I could scarcely believe that the young people who wove those figures and who through the dance lived the old, carefree, spirited life were " hard-core " refugees. After the dancing, they sang their songs — beautiful, haunting songs with melodies that sang in my mind for hours and days, and still try to come back to me.

" If there were nothing else to keep us living, it would be the music that would hold us to life," you said to me.

I sat in the group of your staff people, saw the expressions on their faces as they watched the dancers and listened to the singing, and heard their talking, although I could not understand what they said. They were professors and students well known in your country, you told me. They were teach-

ing here because they were " non-resettleable " in other countries — all of them people of culture and experience, which
was plainly to be seen without your telling me.

As they talked quietly to each other, it was as though they
might be the fathers and mothers of these children, instead of
only their teachers. Or as if you were one close family bound
together by ties deeper even than blood.

That night, you remember, there was the little party in
the room of two young staff people, one of whom is a Lithuanian married to a Russian girl. I had to confess that I had
never in all my life met a Russian, and that I had somewhere
learned to think all Russians were heavy, dark, brooding and
tragic. But here was Kaetke, tiny and graceful, with flaming
red hair and a smile as gay as tomorrow morning. Here was
a Russian girl, married to a Lithuanian, on the staff of a
Lithuanian school for children whose lives had been thwarted
or ruined by what Russia had done to Lithuania, a school in
fact named for Lithuania's independence day. It was as in-
consistent as the little violinist's incongruous repertoire outside my window, yet strangely in keeping with all of you.
You asked Kaetke to sing some of her Russian songs for me,
and for the first time I heard them, as beautiful and tender
and quiet as your own.

" American, Russian, Lithuanian! " you cried. " We are
an international party tonight! "

You asked me to sing my national anthem, but instead of
that I sang a Kentucky mountain ballad. You thought it
sounded like one of your own. I explained that it had come
to America from England.

Suddenly the week, that had seemed so long to look forward to, came to an end. But even the end was unforgettable.
Perhaps you Lithuanians have a custom of making simple

things into important things and simple people into important
ones. Anyway you made an occasion of my departure which
surprised and touched me.

First of all you yourself bundled me determinedly into
that wool scarf and wound it around my neck and head in a
ridiculous way — because you said it was very cold in Finland, and there must not be a recurrence of " the mump." I
was annoyed, partly because it would have been nice for all
you nice people to see me just one time looking somewhat
human. But mostly it was because I knew you needed that
scarf yourself. I refused to take your gift until I saw the
tears that sprang again to your eyes.

" Please forgive me! " you said quickly. " I would like
to tell you in this one little minute a story, just before you go.
It is one that is famous and I think you know it already. It
is about the king who sat in the palace window, and the
beggar who stood outside and asked for alms. The servant
said to the king, ' Oh, my lord King, see the poor beggar who
asks for a penny that he may live! ' And the king said, ' I
will give him something better than a penny! ' The king took
off his coat and hat and handed them to the servant, and without a covering for his head he went into the street. The king
then held out his hand to the beggar and said, ' My friend, I
beg of you, give me money, that I may live! ' Now the
beggar was surprised. But then he smiled! He had some
pennies in his ragged pocket, and he took them and gave them
to the king. And his heart was light again. ' Thank you! '
said the beggar to the king. ' Thank you for making it possible for me to give. Now I am alive again! ' "

I kept the scarf.

While we waited in the courtyard for the car to take me
away, you all began to surround me there. The staff members came, and then the children from the school building,

class by class, the accordion-player with his accordion, and the violinist with his small fiddle. Your principal stood on the steps and made a speech in Lithuanian, while you whispered the translation in my ear. " He thanks you for coming, and thanks you for being sick, although he is sorry you were sick! He asks you to take the greetings of the School of February Sixteenth to the Americans! " He had brought his book of stories and the secretary had brought a book about Lithuania, signed by the staff, and the weaving class had brought a magnificent bookmarker with words in English — " Remember Lithuanian School " — woven into it.

I was overwhelmed. You gave too much. You gave more than you had to give, more than was needed. But then I knew of course that it was needed — it was all needed very much.

Suddenly everyone was silent, and in that crowd of men and women and two hundred children there was not one sound except the quiet slipping of the rope, while your flag was raised on the flagpole, green and yellow and red, like the spring in Lithuania. Slowly it climbed to the top of the pole while you all saluted it. And then your national anthem burst forth and you sang. You all sang!

I could scarcely speak, but just before the car left I did manage to whisper a few words to you before I rode away from the Lithuanian School of February Sixteenth.

I asked you again it you would let me know when Giedra spoke and tell me what she said. Again, you promised to let me know.

My dear Tatjana, I do not think that all Lithuanians are as good as you are, or as generous, tolerant, and forgiving. Surely some of the things you told me were ideas out of your own unusual mind and heart, and you would have had them if you were German, or Russian, or American. But I believe that as long as there is even one Lithuanian with those ideas, your people have a sound, warm " core," and if there were only one person in the world with those ideas, it would mean that the world is well worth keeping.

So I am grateful to all your people there, but to you especially, for more than kindness. We shall learn from you. And we shall wait with eagerness and fear to know whatever words she will say — when Giedra speaks again.

FROM FINLAND

CHAPTER TWENTY-FIVE

Green Gold

I had some high resolves pending my visit to Finland and its northernmost state, Lapland. One of these was that I'd come back prepared to describe this country, and its scenery and its people, with some word a little more specific than " wonderful." Yet now I find myself stuck with that word. The scenery, the food, the people — wonderful!

" But those people," my friends ask me; " are they poor? Some of them are refugees from the war, aren't they? "

I stop to think. " Refugees " doesn't seem quite the word, although technically many thousands of Finnish people did leave the eastern part of the country (Karelia and Petsamo on your map) which was claimed by Russia after the war. And nearly every family in Lapland lost its home when the northern part of Finland was burned by the retreating German army according to the " scorched-earth " strategy.

" In a way you'd call many of them refugees," I admit. " But no — the Finns I met are not poor people. I don't know how to tell you. They haven't any money. But they are very rich."

And then I give up. There is no way of telling about the Finnish people. There is no way of describing this apparently simple, and I believe mature, civilization. It is incredible. It must be something like heaven. But it's a hard life, and cold, too. The people are incredible. They must be something like angels, although they don't look like angels and some of them do get drunk. When I try to tell about Finland and the Finns, I'm frustrated with superlatives and contradictions, and finally reduced to silence.

But I can tell some fragments of stories about places and customs and little things that happened while I was there, in the season of the midsummer midnight sun, which must be very different from the long, long night of snow.*

It is midsummer, and we are in an airplane rising above Helsinki, the White City of the North. With speed that ought to be forbidden, we are out and away and flying now over the Bay of Bothnia, north to Kemi. I wish I could be a camera to photograph forever the fast-moving scene below me — the sea chopped up into little shining strips, by chunks of dark spots that are earth — lonely spots, as lonely and unpeopled and unknown as the sky, the difference being only that one is above looking down instead of below looking up. One has a strange feeling of power and helplessness, knowledge and ignorance, pride and humility.

Once a boy asked me, " What would you think if you were God and made a world and now you were up there looking at what you made? " If I were God and had made a world, and right now were looking down on the Bothnian corner of it, I might be thinking how all this is mine — but it is not mine either because it is its own. The sea, the land, the lonely is-

* My companion and interpreter on this journey was Miss Edith Lonnquist, of Helsinki. In order not to interrupt the stories I have not referred often to Miss Lonnquist, but I would like to call attention to the fact that it was she who planned the journey, guided me all the way, and interpreted not only the conversation of the people I met, but the feelings of the Finnish people as a whole, in a wonderfully helpful manner.

I should like also to acknowledge the hospitality offered by the Finnish YWCA and the Ministry of Social Welfare, through their officers, Miss Helmi Dahlstedt, and Mr. Niilo Kotilainen of Helsinki and Mr. Reino Sarvola of Rovaniemi, and finally the financial help of the Christian Children's Fund, directed by Dr. J. Calvitt Clarke, of Richmond, Virginia.

lands, the whole world around, each person like a lonely island of consciousness, knowing little, knowing not even itself — every piece moving, living, growing, according to a pattern and a rule which I must understand because I made it. But, not being God and not having made the world, I am frightened and lonely looking down on the Bothnian Bay.

I remember the landing at Kemi. It is nine o'clock in the evening, but it is not even dusk. It is as light as it was in the early afternoon. A few people riding by on bicycles look lonely too. The airplane landing there seems alien. It does not belong. I see a dark forest and a river jammed with logs — Finland's " green gold," I am told. One can never forget the logs, for they ride every swift river in Finland, bumping against each other, or marching downstream in endless processions. They give one a feeling of timelessness. There is never any end of them, there is never any cessation of the motion as long as one looks. As long as one looks there is the rolling river, carrying with it the moving parade of logs.

I remember the miles of blackened land, telling of the inferno that swept across those many miles a few years ago. And I remember the new forests planted over the old, growing quickly, fresh new green against the black. " You can burn, but you cannot destroy this land," they say. I remember the new, new buildings, for there is nothing old in Lapland, in towns that are as modern as tomorrow. They too shout that here are a people who simply will not die. The black land, the young green, the very architecture of the buildings, are mysteries as deep as the lonely islands in the Bothnian Bay, and deep as the long, long night, and the summer sun that never goes down.

I remember the motorboats slipping through quiet, shining lonely spaces, through changing pictures, a silent movie.

What kinds of people could live and share such mysteries?

Would they be fearful or fearless?   Sturdy or weak?   Generous or niggardly?   Stolid or humorous?   Mystical or realistic?   Remembering or forgetting?

One wonders what kind of person he would be if he lived in this country.

CHAPTER TWENTY-SIX

Posti Auto to Inari

We are riding a *posti auto* from Rovaniemi (the capital city of Lapland) up to Inari, in the far north, and there is almost no place farther north to go, in this country. After Inari we must take a motorboat across a lake to get to our destination, which is Riutula orphanage. I am speculating a little on that motorboat ride, through a lake that was ice-bound two weeks ago. It will be cold, and I hate to be cold. But I am not speculating very much because the *posti auto,* and the passengers, and the miles of Lapland through which we are jouncing and bumping on seats without springs — all these have immediate importance.

The yellow *posti auto* makes the rounds of every isolated small village in this part of the northland, delivering the mail. The regular commercial buses are more comfortable, the seats have springs, and they are less crowded. I believe the fare is slightly higher, and they follow the scenic ways. But most of the Finnish people take the *posti auto* because it goes often and makes all the stops.

Our conveyance, therefore, is crowded. Among the passengers are two young Finnish vacationers studying maps. Their bicycles are hanging on the rack on the back of the bus. There is a blonde schoolteacher who knows enough English to say, " Welcome to Lapland," but that is all. There is a big Lapp family all in costume. The women wear red bonnets with long ears, and black full skirts with gay embroidered borders and belts. The men wear the four-pointed tam-o'shanter, each point representing one of the four winds. The little girls and the little boys are colorful replicas of their elders. There is a Lapp postman who isn't wearing the costume. When asked why, he says that as postman in Lapland, he must travel to so many places where the Lapp dress is a curiosity to tourists that in earlier days when he wore the costume his time was consumed with inquiries about it. Now he does not wear the costume, but his time, he says, is still consumed by inquiries from people who look at him (and no doubt note the unmistakable Lapp features, high cheek bones, narrow black eyes, and round grin) and ask him why he is *not* wearing the Lapp costume.

There is a young man, a social worker on his way to Utsjoki. He has two big photograph albums with him, and is eager to show us the pictures of Utsjoki in midwinter. While looking at pictures of ice-bound winter in the far north, and riding northward through young forests starting up over charred miles of earth, I see Lapland in midsummer — not less wonderful because, as the hands on my watch go on to seven and eight and nine and ten, it is still noon all around us. When we stop at the little towns we see people riding on bicycles, drinking coffee, standing about, or walking about, as if it weren't bedtime. There is not much sleeping in Lapland, they tell me, in summer.

All the passengers, hearing a strange tongue, as conversation is translated to me by the interpreter who shares my journey, listen with wonder and amusement. Apparently the English language sounds absurd. Even the bus driver is interested, and soon we are all one party. In spite of being three thousand miles from home — in a strange land where every word I understand must come to me through an interpreter — I now feel very much at home. It is an odd feeling, to be at home in Finland, for one is never unconscious of the differences between his own land and this one, his own people and these. Nonetheless one is confident. One is more confident than in New York where everybody speaks English. One's safety, and his pocketbook, and more than that his innate dignity as a human being, are all assured in Finland, I believe.

As we go careening along, turning from vista to forest, and never far from a lake on one side or the other, I am presently aware of a slight stir among the passengers, and a feeling that something unusual — not alarming, but unusual — is about to happen. The interpreter believes we must be going in the wrong direction. The other passengers think so too, but are not disturbed. My interpreter makes her way up to the front of the bus to consult the driver, and comes back to our rear seat, smiling.

" It is nothing," she assures me. " Nothing is wrong. It is only that the bus driver wishes an American to see more of Lapland. He has left the regular route in order to take his bus up to the top of the highest mountain in this region so that you may look at a view from there. He is sure that you will like to see the view."

Up and up we climb. It is not exactly as one climbs a mountain, because here is only a broad, long slope, but it is soon apparent that we are very high indeed, because we have passed the tree line, into bare miles of space, and then the snow line, and after that we are surrounded on either side of the road by snow banks — in midsummer.

We come at last to a stop on top of the world. Again it is not a breathtaking top, but is more like the surface of a round ball looking out over the gently rounded tops of other balls, each one circled with plains and small lakes, and down in the distance the beginning of the trees.

Everybody gets out and walks around, enjoying the off-track excursion as much as I do. With my camera I take pictures of the bus driver, the Lapp postmaster, the social worker, and some others. We go inside the little campers' hut of logs, and see the small cot, the shelf with a few dishes on it, two chairs, the fireplace with a fire carefully laid for the next people who will use the hut, and who will, before leaving there, lay the fire carefully again, and wash and stack the dishes for the ones to follow. There is a guest book on the window sill, in which all of us travelers sign our names.

" You're certainly a hospitable people! " I exclaim, and when this remark is interpreted among them, the bus passengers smile and nod, accepting the tribute for all of Finland. After a leisurely look around we all climb back into the *posti auto* to return to the regular route and continue our journey to Inari.

But hospitality breeds hospitality. A few miles farther along the way, the bus stops again. I learn that there is another place of interest which our driver thinks an American would like to see. It is a bear's cave, not directly on the road, but some distance up the hill. The bear's cave has a story which all Lapland knows.

But first I must ask about something else. For I have seen, although nobody called my attention to it, there at the beginning of the trail, a neat grave, bordered with round firm stones, and at its head a cross of wood, and hanging over the top of the cross an iron helmet. Beyond the grave, on the other side of the road, there is a charred field, just beginning to show green again, through the black cinders. New trees have not yet been planted here.

" It is a lovely grave," I remark, " and in a nice place at the foot of the hill. But it's a lonely grave."

" It is the grave of a German soldier," I am told. " That is a German helmet hanging on the cross."

I am confused. I haven't heard correctly, perhaps.

" But wasn't it the German army that burned all of that forest? " I ask. " Didn't the Germans burn all of Lapland's ' green gold ' during the war? "

They agree. Some add, " And the buildings also. All the buildings were burned as well. There are no old buildings in Lapland because they were burned by the German army during the war."

" Then why would there be a German grave in Lapland back here in the hills, so carefully tended? " I persist. " It seems very odd to me."

" The Finns are perhaps odd people," they admit. " But it is not strange to us. And it is not uncommon. Wherever a German soldier was found dead, his body was buried in this way in a grave. Of course it is cared for. It is our custom to care for the resting places of the dead. It is not strange at all."

I save that to think about later on. Now another small thing is bothering me.

" How can the helmet stay there? " I ask. " Why is it some traveler, some camper hasn't carried it home for a souvenir? "

That, interpreted, makes everybody smile, as if they thought I were joking. But I am not joking.

I learn then about the " law of the land." This, as I understand it, means simply that any article left on a roadside — or left anywhere in this strange country — belongs, until its original owner comes to claim it, to the spot where it is laid. No one will take it away — the ax, the bicycle, the camera, whatever it may be. It stays there, simply because that is the " law of the land." It follows that the helmet, which belonged to the German soldier, will not be removed through all time from the spot where he left it.

" But after all, the German is dead! " I exclaim. " He never will come back after the helmet. It doesn't really belong to him any more, does it? "

" Perhaps not," is the answer. " But regardless of whether he comes or not, the helmet still does not belong to anybody else."

" Well, I can't understand it," I say. " And I can't really believe it either."

" It is not so difficult to understand," I am assured. " It is perhaps a different way of looking at things. You may become accustomed to the idea that what is found belongs to the finder. We see it the other way. Regardless of how the article got to the place, it remains that the article is not mine. Therefore I do not touch it. It is very simple. But now — the cave."

I am not exactly ready to toss off two important philosophical questions so easily, and also I am conscious of the hour. I ask if the bear's cave might make us too late to the next station stop.

" Late? " the driver is bewildered. " There is plenty of time," he says. " All the time there is! "

We are on our way to the bear's cave.

The cave is fully a quarter of a mile up the hill, a steep one this time. I could easily manage the climb independently, but it is the pleasure of the driver to pull one arm, and the Lapp postmaster to haul the other, and between them I am carried up the trail. In the course of pulling and hauling I hear the story.

Once upon a time a Lapp was out hunting, and as evening came on — it not being the season of midnight sun — and it was about to be dark, the Lapp looked for a shelter for the night. He soon discovered a cave — the very cave, as it happened, that we are now climbing up to see. He crawled inside, found a carpet of pine needles and reindeer moss, and went to sleep. A little later a bear came along, also seeking shelter. This was perhaps the cave where the bear was accustomed to sleep. Anyway the bear at once crawled in, lay down on the pine-needle bed, and went promptly to sleep too. The next morning when the Lapp was about to wake, he felt something warm and furry cuddling against him. Opening his eyes he saw that he had been sleeping with a bear.

That is the end of the story. Presumably the Lapp arrived safely home to tell it. I like to imagine, however, a more folksy Finnish ending. I believe the Lapp might have observed to the bear, when they both awakened that morning, something like this, " Well, good morning. Since we have slept together peacefully we should part peacefully also. If you, therefore, will put away your claws, I will put away my gun — so — and say, ' Farewell, and God go with you.' "

The Finns, being strictly honest, give the story no such ending, but I think it could have been so among people like these.

My escorts point out the hole close to the ground where the Lapp crawled in, and the bear crawled in. They suggest that I crawl in also. I do, to find a room higher than my head, an ample bed chamber, somewhat dark and shadowy.

" It is big enough, is it not, for a man and a bear to sleep in together? " they ask anxiously.

I agree that it is big enough, and also remark that it is a hospitable cave, for there is a visitors' book on the shelf of rock. I sign my name in the visitors' book of the bear's cave, and we start on the trail back down to the bus. The passengers waiting in the bus are eager to know how the American liked the bear's cave, and are pleased that I am pleased. We go on.

We arrive at the next post stop an hour late. The little

crowd waiting there to get on the bus ask why. The driver explains. They are delighted. Everybody shakes hands around. The ones who are leaving us here — the school-teacher and the postmaster, and the Lapp family — wish us good fortune.

We go on to Inari.

CHAPTER TWENTY-SEVEN

Lastenkoti in Lapland

Inari is a small town on the edge of a vast lake. There is a romantic tale about a voice long ago which moaned out from the depths of the lake, saying, " As deep as it is wide! " " As deep as it is wide! "

We are met at the water's edge by a boat which looks like any rowboat to me, except for the small engine at one end, and we are stowed away in the bottom of the boat and snugly tucked in sheep-lined coats provided by a cheerful motorman, sent to meet us by the Riutula *lastenkoti* (orphanage). The motorman wears a sheep-lined jacket too, and a fur cap, and stands by his motor smiling confidently. I hope that he is as skilled as he seems confident.

The engine begins to make some choking gasping noises, there is some uneven *put-putting*, and then we skim suddenly away from the good safe shore, out onto the shining surface of the lake. Our boat seems small and alone on the big surface of that lake. I dare not think how cold the water is, two weeks ago ice-locked, and I dare not remember the voice that moaned from the depths, " As deep as it is wide! "

Our boat gathers speed. The *put-putting* is more frequent and regular. It becomes a steady roar, as we move more and more swiftly. I force myself to consider harmless colorful bits such as how late the hour is. My watch says eleven o'clock, and officially it is nighttime. I consider how light the world is all around us. Broad daylight, yet daylight with a mocking awareness of the fact that it ought to be dark.

The minutes skim along with us. After a while I have lost track of time, half-lulled to sleep by the roar, by the surrounding silence, by the distant shores, which seem instead of ourselves to be speeding along — shadowy, lonely shores, covered with dark hemlock forests, and never a house, never a barn, never even a clearing that we can see. So quickly does one freeze into this human will to resist change that it is almost a shock when we at last approach the farther side of the lake.

But now there is in sight a clearing, and a farmhouse on the hill, and down close to the lake a little log building which by this time I know is the *sauna*. I experience an instant of terror, knowing that the first entertainment to be offered, even in an orphanage, will doubtless be a steam bath. It's a fearful prospect to the novitiate, but it's hospitality one dare not refuse.

The farmhouse is the Riutula orphanage. I have heard a few things about it — that there are about twenty children there, most of them Lapps, that a number of them are " children of war," and that their orphanage mother is a Lutheran Deaconess, Miss Annikki Multanen.

As we come nearer and nearer, and at last are there, unbelievably making the soft *plop* against the shore, miraculously rescued somehow one more time out of eternity, I see the crowd of little boys and girls, most of them wearing red bonnets and pointed tam-o'shanters, all with round dark faces, so different from the blonde Finns I have seen in the south. They are crowding about, and hiding behind the long ample skirts of the plump small rosy woman who must be Miss Multanen. She has on a Lapp bonnet, although she's plainly Finnish, and wears high boots. She looks rather old, but she moves spryly.

Half a moment after the welcomes and the introductions

are done, she assures us eagerly, " I have just made up the fire, with the help of these boys. The *sauna* is all ready for you now! "

The orphanage, the children, everything in the new world will come later. We are hurled first of all into the *sauna*.

This *sauna* is difficult to describe. But it is important, because it means so much to the Finnish people. It has perhaps some connection with Finnish cleanliness in general, which seems to me right on a level with, if not just a notch ahead of, godliness.

Miss Multanen, Miss Lonnquist, the interpreter, and I go down to the log hut together. The children have had their *sauna*, and their *sauna* " party " which always follows, and are now on their way to bed. We are first, and after us the old Lapp caretaker, who is the only man on the place, will have the *sauna* for as long as he likes. " He might stay there all night," Miss Multanen says. " It is where he thinks and dreams, that old man! " In earlier days, she tells me, the men and women were all together in the *sauna*. Now they go separately.

We go into the first room of the small two-room hut. There is a blazing open fire in the fireplace, and the room is so hot that at first I have trouble in getting my breath. But this is not the " hot " room. It is only the undressing room. There are benches around the sides where we may sit and talk while we're taking off our clothes. There is no hurry. This *sauna* is not a matter of minutes, but an hour, or hours, and it is a social occasion too. We get acquainted.

I'm uncomfortable, in spite of trying to be nonchalant and do as the Romans, about this disrobing in company. The other women tell me most Americans are. They say it's false modesty and they can't understand why people should be ashamed of their bodies. If you're unbaring your soul, that might be different. But bodies are bodies! They remark that Americans *aren't* truly so very well developed, and that may be because we diet all the time. I repeat to myself that a bath just doesn't need to be sociable; nonetheless I put off the moment for the hot room as long as I can, by being social.

And then, since sometime it must come, I go cautiously over to the door and take a courageous peek into the " hot " room. I jump back in dismay. This is the hottest room I've ever felt. No human being could live in such heat. The others laugh and tell me to go on in. I'm sure I shall die, but I can't permit these Finnish women, who are already comparing (in Finnish) my inadequate physique with their well-developed frames, to think Americans are weaklings. I grit my teeth and " go on in."

When I can get my breath and take a look around, and when I get used to the half darkness in there — for there is only a tiny window — I see in one corner a tub of water, and in another a structure of tin or iron, which looks like a stove. There are coals at the bottom, and hot rocks fill it up to the top. On the other side of the small room there are tiers of seats, like bleachers, but broader, climbing up to the low ceiling. The stronger one is the higher he goes, for of course it's hottest up close to the ceiling.

I take the lowest bench, to start with, and they hand me a bunch of birch leaves — the " bouquet " they call it — and tell me I'm supposed to beat myself with that. Beat myself! I mutter, " Horrible! " but under my breath. And it does seem to be good exercise, on experiment. I'm beginning to get used to the heat, and to perspire. It doesn't seem so bad. I rather like the whole thing.

But then, just as I'm getting cozy, Miss Multanen dashes a small pan of water over the hot rocks in the stove, and a volcano erupts. The room is white with steam. I'm suffocated. I squeeze my eyes shut, and gasp, and scream, and although I can't see them through the steam I can hear them laughing at me. I think I must certainly be dying, and sink down onto my bench to wait for the end. But then the steam melts away in the air, and I'm still alive and sweating rivers. Miss Multanen and Miss Lonnquist are on the top bench beating themselves enthusiastically. I try a feeble imitation, but without any enthusiasm.

With all that I'm worn out. They stay up there on the top row singing songs and chatting in Finnish, and occasionally shouting to me in English. It's as gay as if we'd always known each other. I lie on my low bench dripping and languid (for hours and hours it seems), not wanting to move.

At last the steam part is over. I'm still not eager to move, but the others leap down from the ceiling, and dip out pans of water from the big tub. This is for us to have a real wash off with soap. By the time the birch leaves and the perspiration are washed away, I feel several pounds less, and dehydrated.

We go back to the dressing room, which was so hot to begin with, and now seems frigid. There's a quick rubdown with a towel, and I hover over the bright fire, while Miss Multanen stands in the open doorway without a stitch on, fanning herself. Then we dress and get ready to leave the hut. When we strike the icy air outdoors I think we must make little clouds of steam around us, walking up the hill. I feel like a stove, walking.

The children are all in bed. Except for the glimpse of a few of them when we arrived, we haven't seen anything of this Lapland orphanage family, but Miss Multanen tells us we'll make their acquaintance tomorrow. Now we have our " *sauna* party " in front of the open fire in the living room. Over coffee and bread and margarine and reindeer meat and exciting little sweetcakes which she has made herself in the big wood range in the kitchen, we talk about the *sauna.*

" How do you feel now? " she asks me.

" I feel clean — and warm! " I assure her.

" Did you like the *sauna?* Was it all right? " she inquires eagerly, anxiously. It is important that I should like it. And now that it's over, and I'm warm all through and vibrating, and as clean as I've ever been in my life, I find to my great surprise that I do like it. I love it!

" There is nothing in Finland that is so Finnish as the *sauna,*" she tells me earnestly.

The next morning (it has never been night, but we have gone to bed and slept), I meet the children — Nielo, and Anni, and Jan, and Helmi, and all the others. They are beautiful children, the Lapps, their brown slant eyes as bright as their bonnets. And I see now that some of the Riutula children are Finnish too, with flaxen hair and soft blue eyes.

I can't talk with these children, even through the interpreter, for they are shy. They are much more timid than the youngsters I have met in the other parts of Europe. I remember that they have lived here in a lonely place all their lives, and have met very few strangers. They cling close to Miss Multanen, and hide behind her staring at me with great curiosity. As she pulls them out to be introduced to me they shake hands awkwardly, and then run. Some of the older boys click their right heels against the left and bow. It's a Finnish custom. And then they run too, fleet as deer, out of the room. But I know they are watching us from a safe place behind the door.

They all look glowingly healthy.

" But what if there should be sickness here? " I ask. " Is there any doctor near by? "

Miss Multanen tells us that the nearest doctor is at Inari,

on the other side of the lake. In winter they can reach him on skates or skis, or they can take a reindeer *pulkka*. And in summer they can go to Inari in the boat. But it's a long journey. Fortunately they don't really need a doctor here. There is seldom any sickness. There has not been any sickness here for two years running. And in case of small accidents or upset stomachs, or bad colds, she herself is the doctor.

" There was the time when Hillike's arm was broken," she recalls smiling. " That was difficult. The ice was just breaking and there was no way to get to Inari at all. But it was not so bad either, because I could talk to the doctor on the telephone. While one of these children held the telephone for me to hear his directions, I set the broken bone in exactly the way he described, and adjusted the sling for it. And it was all right."

I want to see Hillike's arm, repaired by telephone. It is as straight and strong as the other one.

" He is a great one for skiing! " she says. " It would have been bad to lose the use of the arm! "

Miss Multanen calls my attention to the neat schoolhouse above, some distance away from the orphanage farm. It is empty now because this is the summer holiday, but in the winter the children will have classes there. This is the only school for the county, and those children who come from homes far away must be boarders, because they cannot go back and forth through the snow.

The interpreter goes on to tell me how, after the war, and the burning of Lapland by the German army, and the return of the people who had fled, the first buildings to rise again were the schools. After that came the hospitals, and finally the homes and offices and stores. The schools, being most important, came first, and there is not a county anywhere in Lapland which does not have its new school.

I wonder about the future of these children. Most of the boys will be lumbermen or farmers, I am told, but there will also be builders and mechanics among them. A few will go on to school, perhaps finally even to the university at Helsinki. But the most important thing is that whatever they choose as their jobs, they must all be prepared to be useful citizens of a country which needs its people to be strong and industrious and honest.

I know that a good many of these children are orphans from the war, in one way or another, and inquire about their backgrounds. This is the first question which Miss Multanen seems to hesitate about answering. Or perhaps she is a little annoyed.

" Of course," she says, " they are homeless children, or they would not be here. Of course there was tragedy for them. Of course there was war for their parents."

But she does not seem to wish to discuss these tragedies.

" It is all in the past," she says. " It has nothing to do with the present. And now we are in the present. We look forward to the future. The present is warm and kind. The future must be full of hope. If you do not hope, what is the use of living? If you are always looking backward, how can you go ahead? It is really very simple."

Deaconess Multanen interests me a great deal. I had thought when I saw her first that she was an old woman. But when she takes off her bonnet, I see that her hair is not gray but blonde, and she is really quite young. When she takes off her glasses she is very pretty. The red in her cheeks is natural.

I look at the books in her bookcase. There are a few classics, a few very modern books. Some of them are English and American novels translated into Finnish. Some are in English, although Miss Multanen does not speak English.

There are books on co-operatives, on government, on psychology, and child care. I see that she has a record player, and some excellent albums of records. We discuss the Sibelius Week which has just ended. She also heard the *Finlandia* broadcast on her radio.

I look at the pictures on the wall, several good oil paintings. They look familiar, and learning that she does a little painting herself I conclude that these are pictures of scenes about Riutula. I see the photographs (all Finnish homes have photograph albums) and can see that Miss Multanen is a skier and skater. She looks well on skis too.

Altogether this is no dull grandmother of a little person, cozily salted away in an old farmhouse, just sheltering a lot of unfortunate little orphans. Here is a young, scholarly woman, who could go anywhere, discuss any subject with almost anybody. She would be at home in Helsinki or New York or London.

I want to ask her if she doesn't get lonely here for somebody who speaks her language. I know that she has a co-worker, and a few other helpers. But she must be much alone. I think she's wasted back here in the Styx. After I've said all this to the interpreter, not intending for it to be translated, I realize that although Miss Multanen doesn't speak much English, she understands it far too well, and has understood what I have said. I am embarrassed. I remember too that Miss Multanen is a Lutheran Deaconess, which means that her life is a formally dedicated one. I wish she hadn't understood what I said.

She is apparently a little nonplussed, but perhaps writes it off as another queer Americanism. We probably have a reputation for minding others' affairs for them. But she is Finnish and courteous. She smiles, and tries to answer me.

" There are not many people here or living near here,"

she admits. " But generally when there is a Finnish farm home, there is a family reading the newspapers, listening to the radio, knowing the news, and good music. Generally there are young people who have attended the folk high schools where they learn how to make their living in the country, and how to live better lives. They are artists and musicians and thinkers and even politicians. They think of how to work for their people, for each other, for their country. Life is never tiresome if you can think, and see, and worship. We are fed by the few visits we have with each other so that we are full for the weeks and months when there can be no visits. And I am very busy. No, I should say that life is never dull, as you say. But the most important thing is to have your job to do, to know that it is your job, and to learn every day to do it better than yesterday."

While she has talked in this way the children have been coming back into the room, reassured by the steady hum of our voices, perhaps, and lured by the curious sound of the English. Two little ones have climbed into her lap. The rest sit on the floor by her chair, or stand there holding onto it while she rocks gently back and forth. She doesn't make a fuss over them, or even seem to notice them very much. There is no extravagant show of affection. (I think Miss Multanen must have studied her books on child psychology.) There is complete acceptance on both sides. Quietly they love and trust each other.

" Here is my job," she says. " I consider it worth while."

Afterward I reflect that we didn't ever get to the subject I had come a long way to discuss with a Finnish orphanage superintendent — the war. I know that a number of these youngsters are " children of war," having lost one or both parents in the war. I know that some are from families that moved west from Petsamo when Russia occupied that section of Finland. I know that all of them are from families whose homes were burned by the German army. I know that at least one is the child of a Lapp woman and a German soldier. I know that one is the child of a Finnish soldier who died, and a Finnish mother who lost her mind because of those war experiences, and is now in a mental institution.

How do they think? How do they feel? I have no answer to that, for I am always magicked away from the subject of war, poverty, loss and frustration, when I try to discuss them with these Finns. They require that they be permitted to live, and to build in the present, and to plan for the future. I think perhaps they require also to be permitted to have done with the past. That is that.

CHAPTER TWENTY-EIGHT

Very Simple—Very Practical

We have returned by motorboat and *posti auto* to Rovaniemi, which is the capital city of this wonderland of Lapland. Rovaniemi is small, and reminds me in some ways of a frontier town, but it is the most modern city I have ever seen. It is brand, startlingly new, like an architect's drawing for the world of the future. It is like a collection of sparkling stones, freshly cut, that one might hold in his hands and examine, one by one, line by line. The small white store buildings, the cinema building, the small bright restaurants, the office buildings, the hotel by the river, are all *fresh*. The small church on the hill, white, simple, almost forbidding in its plainness outside, has a modern interior too, like no other church sanctuary I have ever seen. There are bright murals lining both sides. The pictures are from the Scriptures, and the verses below — in Finnish — Bible verses; but the figures pictured are all of Lapp people. Jesus, talking to the children, is a Lapp, talking to Lapp boys and girls, who wear bonnets and four-pointed caps. Although I cannot read it, I know that the verse below says, " Suffer the little children to come."

A whole new city. Nothing old! " But it isn't exactly a cozy town," I tell myself.

I remember that this city hadn't a chance to grow up year after year, changing its size and form and coloring from building to new building through generation after generation. The old Rovaniemi was burned to the ground by the

German army in 1944. The new one is rising quickly over ashes. And yet it is not unsubstantial as such quick growth is likely to be. Everything built in Finland is solid, built to stay, I am told. Not one shattering memory of the past will tempt a Finn to build for the moment, in fear that what he builds today may be captured or destroyed tomorrow.

The hotel where I am staying is an example of functional elegance. The furniture in my room is composed of a plain Hollywood bed, a shining wing chair, severe lamps. The Finnish birch makes lovely furniture which needs neither paint nor stain nor elaborate lines to decorate it. The draperies at the window are plain and straight. It is all simple, substantial, smart, and ultra-modern, every corner and stitch.

Outside, just under my window, the river flows swiftly along. Any time in the night I may waken to look at it, because it is light all night. And the river never stops. It moves continuously, carrying with it always the vast procession of logs. I find myself dizzily trying to focus my eyes on one log and to follow its course all the way down the stream in an almost frantic effort to see this one scrap of motion somehow completed in a small way. But I never can hold the one log with my eyes. It melts into the great procession, and on they come and on they come. I feel finally as if I were the one who moved — and moved — and the dizzy procession standing still.

The governor's office is on an upper floor of the rather small, simple and elegant building of wood and stucco which is Lapland's State Office Building. We give our names to the man in the first office, and in three minutes we are ushered into Governor Hannula's presence. There is no waiting. There are no secretaries to tell us the governor is in conference, or has been called out suddenly, or will be back this afternoon or next week.

I am prepared to be impressed with the honor of talking to a governor. I am impressed. And yet this man does not look like a governor. He might be any one of the shop people who have been so cordial and informal, and so much interested in helping me here in Rovaniemi. He is rather tall, quite bald, and gentle. He does not look young, but he looks as though he might live forever. This man never left his state at the time it was burned. He has been governor for goodness knows how many years, and will be as long as he lives, because in Finland state governors are elected for life. I think that's strange, but they say it's very simple. They tell me it is their custom to choose the right man for an important job, and to keep him until he dies.

We sit down in some easy chairs at one end of the office, with no imposing official desk between us. I see that this is a visit, not an interview, and I know that with the governor of Lapland I may discuss some of those peculiar little questions which have been bothering me ever since I came here. I relax.

By way of conversation Governor Hannula asks me first of all if I have had *sauna*, whether I liked it, and how I felt after the first one. I tell him that I felt clean, and that I loved it.

" You are kind to like the *sauna*, or to say so! " he says smiling. I realize again that *sauna* is far, far more to the Finns than a bath. " Few Americans do like it at first. But they learn to, I think. And yet you might stay here for many years, and never learn exactly how the Finns feel about the *sauna*."

I say that I have felt this deep importance, but have not realized just why it should be so.

He smiles again.

" It may seem odd to you," he said. " But no one can really understand the Finns until he has first learned about *sauna*. We are perhaps a strange people. But this *sauna* in a way is the center of our culture, our life, our religion. It is physical cleanliness, as you say, and we believe that is important, but it represents also spiritual strength, purity. In the intense heat, in the boiling steam, all the dust and grime of the body, all the bits of the world which have attached themselves to us, are cleansed away. And at the same time all the dark parts of the mind and soul are cleansed away also. All the troubles heaped on us by the world of living people, all the problems of life, are lightened."

He continues to talk, and as it is interpreted, I listen with wonder.

" In a cold country there must be ways of keeping warm. It has always been that way through our history — the struggle of a determined people to live in a hard, cold climate, fighting the long winter, the mountains, the lakes, the rushing rivers, the loneliness, fighting for life itself. Therefore we must be strong. We must be clean. *Sauna* represents the struggle, the reward, the cleanliness. As it has become the part of our stubborn hold on life, it has grown close to our hearts. It is a part of birth, and of death. When the child is about to be born, the mother goes to *sauna* for delivery and the child is first bathed in *sauna*. When he is an old man and it is time for him to die and become a part of eternity, the dead body left behind is carried to *sauna* for its last cleansing on this earth, before it is laid in the grave.

" Sharing so our beginning and our ending on this earth, *sauna* has become the occasion which we share with our nearest and dearest. Together we are cleansed of problems, of worries, of quarrels even. For *sauna* is no casual wash-off, quickly over. It takes a long time, and there is plenty of time too, for cleansing the body of impurities, the mind and heart of evil.

" And it is thus that we offer *sauna* to our guests, the choicest hospitality we have, the best we can give to the stranger. In *sauna* we open our hearts, and invite him to be one of us. And when one is alone — well, I myself have stayed in *sauna* alone for many hours, on occasions, over many years, for it is here that I can think with freedom, the good, clean, ongoing thoughts. Here I can make my truest decisions for my state and my country, which are required of me. I tell you that Finland would not be here today if it were not for the history of cleanliness and strength of body and spirit, that we have in *sauna!* "

Governor Hannula is deeply affected. So am I. I do not quite understand even now, but I am humble.

We are silent for a few minutes. It is not an awkward silence, but one in which we can think. Then I ask a question. It is about the German soldier's grave which I saw on the road to Inari. He nods, as though it were not anything unusual.

" There are many of these in Lapland," he says, " and in southern Finland also.

" We have kept records of those German soldiers who died. Our government has found their names and addresses and has notified their families in Germany. We have invited those families to come to Finland, to visit the resting places of their sons, their husbands and their brothers. When they come we welcome them." He smiles. " We even invite them to *sauna!* "

" But that's what I don't understand," I interrupt. " I can't understand your taking so much trouble for the Germans. They burned Lapland. They were your enemies then, weren't they? "

" They are not our enemies any more," he says mildly. " They are immortal souls! "

We are both silent again.

" It — it's a new idea. I'm trying to understand it," I say finally.

" It is not strange," he assures me. " It is very simple. We are practical people here. We have much to get done. We have a new state to build in Lapland, over the burned places. We cannot spend time in wars that are done, whether we won or lost. It takes too much time to study about revenge. We can't build, and go ahead, if we must look back and hate. We have no time for continuing the war, either the one with the Germans or the one with the Russians, even with our minds. That is all. It is the only practical way."

And then he changes the subject.

" What do you think of the building we have done here, may I ask? What do you think of our new towns, our health centers, our hospitals, our children's homes, our homes for aged people, our co-operatives? What do you think of the new Lapland? "

I cannot say in a word, because I have no word big enough, but he seems to be satisfied.

" Our people must be healthy," he says. " We have spared no expense in building our health centers all through this state, and our hospitals are as well equipped as any in the world, I think. We have built all our schools. We have children's homes. Our children we must care for first be-cause they must become strong citizens if we are to have a strong land. Our old people — well, they have worked hard! We honor them now by helping them to be healthy and happy and comfortable."

He chuckles.

" Some of our old Lapp people do not like the new homes very much. They have never slept in beds. Do you know what we do for them? We permit them to lay their reindeer skins on the floor and sleep on them as they always have done. It is better, when one is old, to live as one likes."

He laughs, and I do too, remembering the fine modern Lapp home for the aged which I visited near Inari, and the old Lapp people who live there, not so severely as they have lived in their youth, but enjoying still most of their old customs and costumes and habits. I remember the old women smoking their pipes in great peace, and eating the reindeer meat which they like so much.

But I have another question.

" It is very expensive, this building program," I say. " And I know that you have lost much in the various wars you've had. I wonder that you have the courage to use your ' green gold ' to build so strongly for a future, when — excuse me — we both know there is a chance of there not *being* any future, for your buildings."

I am surprised that he is not irritated. He nods thoughtfully, seeming to agree with me.

" There will be a future for our people," he says. " We build. What we build today may be burned tomorrow. We plant. Tomorrow our forests may be burned. It has happened before. But if our building and our planting are burned, we will, as soon as we can, build and plant again. We are not afraid of war, or invading armies. We do not spend the little money we have in preparing for war, as you spend your vast sums of money for that purpose in America. Even if we spent all that we have on arms and armies we should still be powerless to resist the strength of a larger nation turned against us. Our only defense is to keep from having enemies if we can. We have not enough money to build an army, as I say, but we have enough money to build a people, and to keep our people strong. As long as we have our people we are a state. The forests we can always plant again. The buildings we can build again. In the meantime, today, we plant, and we build well, for it is not right to build any other way."

I thank him for what he has said to me, and looking at the clock I remark that I've taken a good deal of a governor's time.

He smiles again.

" We thank you for coming to Lapland," he says graciously. " As for time — well, there is an old saying we have: ' In Lapland there are plenty of miles, and plenty of time! ' You are welcome, and God go with you to America! "

Appendix

The Division of Education of the American Unitarian Association sponsored the planning of this book. They and the author acknowledge with gratitude the co-operation of the agencies, church boards, and other organizations listed below, which made the book possible. Some of them made generous financial contributions, some offered counsel and guidance, and others provided transportation and lodging for the author in their various centers throughout Europe and the Middle East. Without their help the project could not have been accomplished.

IN THE UNITED STATES AND CANADA
American Council of Voluntary Agencies for Foreign Service, Inc.
20 West 40th Street
New York 18, N.Y.
Acting Chairman: Clarence E. Pickett

American Middle East Relief, Inc.
350 Fifth Avenue
New York 1, N.Y.
Executive Director: George Barakat

Children to Palestine, Inc.
1819 Broadway
New York 23, N.Y.
Executive Director: Rev. Ralph H. Read

Christian Children's Fund, Inc.
108 South Third Street
Richmond, Va.
Executive Director: J. Calvitt Clarke

Congregational Christian Service Committee, Inc.
110 East 24th Street
New York 16, N.Y.
Executive Secretary: Earle C. Ballou

Help Finland, Inc.
300 West 108th Street
New York 23, N.Y.
Executive Director: Mrs. Ester Hietala

Lutheran Resettlement Service
21 East 26th Street
New York 10, N.Y.
Resettlement Executive: Miss Cordelia Cox

Royal Egyptian Embassy
Washington, D.C.
Chargé d'Affaires: Mohamed El Kony

Unitarian Service Committee, Inc.
9 Park Street
Boston 8, Mass.
Executive Director: Thomas Pym Cope

Unitarian Service Committee of Canada, Inc.
48 Sparks Street
Ottawa, Canada
Executive Director: Dr. Lotta Hitschmanova

United Lithuanian Relief Fund of America, Inc.
105 Grand Street
Brooklyn 11, N.Y.
Executive Director: Peter Minkunas

United Nations International Children's Emergency Fund
United Nations
New York
Executive Director: Maurice Pate

IN EUROPE AND THE MIDDLE EAST
American Board of Commissioners for Foreign Missions (Istanbul)
Anatolia College (Salonika)
Casa Materna Orphanage (Naples)

Congregational Christian Service Committee (Athens, Salonika, Naples)

Council of Refugee Agencies Licensed for Operation in Germany (Berlin)

Egyptian Ministry of Foreign Affairs (Cairo, Gaza)

Finnish Ministry of Social Welfare (Helsinki, Rovaniemi)

Office of High Commissioner of Germany (Frankfurt)

Lillie Volkert Kinderheim (Ascona)

Lithuanian School of February Sixteenth (Diepholz)

Lutheran World Federation (Geneva, Frankfurt, Hamburg, Berlin)

Palestinian Arab Refugee Institution (Damascus)

Pierce College (Elleniko)

The Red Crescent (Istanbul)

Royal Egyptian Legation to Lebanon and Syria (Beirut, Damascus)

Unitarian Service Committee (Bremen, Toulouse, St. Goin)

Unitarian Service Committee of Canada (Athens)

United Nations Relief and Works Agency to Palestine Refugees (Beirut, Cairo, Gaza, Amman, Jerusalem, Bethlehem, Jericho)

United States Information Service (Beirut, Damascus)

Young Men's Christian Association (Istanbul)

Young Women's Christian Association (Helsinki)

The writer wishes to express her personal gratitude to the many individuals, in this country and abroad, who shared in the project. Some gave financial help with travel expenses. Many in Europe and the Middle East helped personally in a variety of ways, including hospitality and transportation. Many agency officials gave guidance in and out of office hours and far beyond the line of any official requirements. Only a few of them could be mentioned in the text, but they all had important parts. The writer hopes that this book will justify their interest in its making, and she is grateful to offer a study which is made up of the co-operative vision of so many people.

She wishes also to acknowledge, with deep appreciation, the support of the editor, Sophia Lyon Fahs, who has encouraged and guided every phase of her undertaking except the writing of this sentence.

www.ingramcontent.com/pod-product-compliance
Lightning Source LLC
Chambersburg PA
CBHW022332280326
41934CB00006B/601